Dear Abyss

The FreeBSD Journal *Letters* Column
years 1-6

Michael W Lucas

Tilted
Windmill
Press

Copyright Information

Acknowledgements

My dear Patronizers. I warned you. I warned you, and yet you send me money every month. I appreciate you all, even as I can't understand why. I suspect it's some sort of "vengeance upon civilization" thing.

Kate Ebneter, Stefan Johnson, Maximilian Kühne, Jeff Marraccini, and Phil Vuchetich throw so much cash at me, I thank them in in the ebook and print versions of everything. If you'd like to join them, see https://patronizeMWL.com.

For Liz.

Foreword

One day the FreeBSD Foundation decided to start a journal, which has much the same prospects for success as an author deciding to write an operating system. Cheered by the prospect of witnessing three debacles in a trench coat, I offered heartfelt encouragement. Before the butter cooled on my popcorn, they asked me to join the editorial board.

Well. At least they knew they knew nothing. I accepted, thinking I'd spend most of my time writing scathing emails lambasting their foolishness and explaining that working in open source had badly warped their understanding of copyright law. Then Jim Maurer and the fine folks at S&W Publishing took over the real work. I should have bowed out then, but my juvenile concerns about appearing churlish had not yet completely atrophied.

The Journal had an editorial board meeting the night before BSDCan. Lulled by indifferent sweets and a truly excellent fruit salad, I found myself volunteered to write a letters column.

Technical people with a problem are not going to write to a columnist and beg for a solution. By the time the column comes out, that problem has been trampled by a whole herd of problems. Besides, nobody writes a letters column to ask for advice unless their problem is insoluble and they need a hug, or they already know the answer and want permission to act on their worst impulses. Nobody was going to write me. I had to write both the letters and the answers.

Here's the other problem with an advice column. It needs glue.

Saying "I'll write about FreeBSD stuff" isn't enough. People don't beseech Dear Abby for solutions. They want her soothing voice. Her calmness. Her gentle declarations that *yes, you have a problem* or *have you considered complying with conservative societal norms?* If they wanted detailed, thoughtful discussion of their petty problems they'd write Captain Awkward or Dear Prudence. Each columnist has their own voice, their own attitudes, beliefs and mission. Columnists have goals. And seriously, a Unix letters column? No system administration advice I could offer would survive thirty seconds exposure to the sandblaster of reality.

If you look at the first few columns, you'll see I gave it my best shot. My model was in an unstable solar orbit, however, and starting to skip off the heliosphere. I had nothing beyond snark. I know my craft, and can make almost anything readable, but my only desire was to finish the damn column and get back to writing my stupid little books. A few columns in, I had decided that I would give it one year and quit.

Then my past oozed into my present.

In the 1990s I worked as an academic library periodicals cataloger, also known as a "receiving clerk." Magazines from all over the world poured onto my desk in a manner much like the Internet, if the Internet contained facts. I recorded receipt each issue in the computer and sent them up to the periodicals room.[1]

One of those magazines was the century-old British satirical *Punch*.

The last page of every issue featured *Bargepole*. *Bargepole* could fit more bitter rage into a strict one thousand words than

---

1   This is where I learned the difference between *I love books* and *I want to work with books*. I want to write books. I want you to buy those books. Who cares what happens to them afterwards?

I could cram into a month-long gelato bender, yet I had no doubt of his marrow-deep sincerity. His apoplectic frenzy over the wreckage of post-Thatcher Britain charmed me. I savored every word. When *Punch* was canceled for the capitalist crime of "turning a tidy but not excessive profit," Bargepole had the last word. He even left the last sentence of the column unfinished. Left the world hanging.

I didn't agree with Bargepole. Being an ignorant US kid reading a British pop magazine, I didn't even understand it. But his work was a revelation in how every word could—and should—bleed attitude.

Right after deciding to term limit my column, I discovered that Bargepole's work had been collected in a sketchy hardcover and could be mine for a merely extortionate fee. I told the mortgage to piss off, snagged a copy, and drowned myself in glorious prose. Decades later, I had watched many more BBC murder mysteries, understood more of his craftwork, and was even more delighted. Even the discovery that "Bargepole" was not Bargepole's legal name could not disappoint me. Much. I finished reading this tiny book one morning over breakfast, went upstairs to get to work, went back downstairs to find some pants, and tried again.

Before I could start my real work, though, I had to get the stupid Letters column out of the way. I had no idea how I could trudge through it with all that transcendent prose still echoing in my vacuous skull.

Something happened. Something like falling into a vat at the chemical plant and emerging as a deranged pasty-faced clown. The stupid, annoying, painful Letters column came... *alive.*

After writing over a thousand words in thirty incendiary minutes I stood back, lightly stunned.

It wasn't that I'd copied Bargepole. Any vaguely competent author can shallowly mimic another's style. But those words had resonated within me, and led me to create something uniquely mine. And a revelation.

I couldn't give useful advice about specific parts of FreeBSD.

But I could offer my decades of experience in this appalling field.

Letters columns are short. I could do *anything*. I could play with the language. I could push myself to develop richer prose. I could speak my truth. Sincerely. And columns are disposable. Journals are ephemeral, and technical journals doubly so. People save back issues for reference. Nobody sane dredges through old magazine issues to read the "Letters" column. These pieces would vanish. Obscurity is the ultimate liberty.

Maybe the FreeBSD Journal editorial board would reject the piece, but who cared? It's not like I need fresh fruit *every* year.

To my shock, the column was accepted.

So I went harder, trying to push my language even more fiercely. It became less about FreeBSD and more about trying to survive in this most irrational of careers.

I inflicted a compilation of the first two years on my Patronizers. Outsiders asked if they could buy a copy, so I released the three-year collection *Letters to ed(1)*. They demanded more. Here we are, including those struggling first efforts.

Will I keep doing this? For at least four more years. A title has lurked in my brain for decades, waiting for the correct book to nail it to. A ten-year collection would suit nicely.

And wherever Bargepole is today, I hope that the discovery that he influenced me gives him the delightful apoplectic seizure he so richly deserves.

Publisher's Note

This is a hastily assembled compendium of the first six years of Michael W Lucas' We Get Letters column for the FreeBSD Journal, slathered over with miserly editing and mediocre formatting, and slammed out into public as a dubious money-making ploy.

We recommend neither purchasing nor reading this collection. You'll only encourage him.

1

Hi Michael,

We were brainstorming column ideas for the FreeBSD Journal, and Kode Vicious suggested that you might be willing to handle a "Letters" column for us. People would submit their questions to the Journal, and you'd answer them for us. Any chance you'd be interested?

Best,

George V Neville-Neil

FreeBSD Foundation President

Hi George,

This is a terrible idea. It's just awful. This is the Internet age. Nobody reads letters columns, advice columns, or anything like that. We have Stack Exchange, and all kinds of places for people to beg for advice.

FreeBSD has a whole bunch of places where users can go to get specific help. Help ships with the system, in the man pages. Where a bunch of Unix-like operating systems made this absurd decision to bundle manual pages separately, FreeBSD ships with the manual. Actually, you can't *not* install the manual. You could build a FreeBSD that doesn't include the manual, of course, but to do that means reading a whole bunch of man pages.

People say that the manual isn't a tutorial, and they're right. That's why FreeBSD has the Handbook and a whole bunch of articles. Unlike the man pages, you can choose to not install those on a FreeBSD host. You can browse all of the documentation online at https://docs.freebsd.org, though.

New users can start with the FAQ (Frequently Asked Questions) file, which contains literally dozens of questions and answers. It goes into everything from hardware compatibility to

ZFS, and while some of the gags in "The FreeBSD Funnies" have aged dreadfully—nothing scratches in memory banks these days, they fixed that bug back in 1996—the rest of the document is rock-solid. Looking at it now, I realize just how useful it is to new users. I still remember that feeling of enlightenment when I understood why du(1) and df(1) give different answers for disk space usage. Setting aside an hour to read the FAQ will give new users that enlightened feeling over and over again.

Then there's the Handbook. It's broken up by tasks. If a user's question has a little more depth than what's in the FAQ, the Handbook is there for you. Some of the material orients the reader, and is well worth reading so that new FreeBSD administrators understand why there's so much in /usr/local when everybody else just dumps everything in /etc and /bin.

Plus there's all sorts of FreeBSD-related sites these days. Even my blog has some FreeBSD tutorials on it.

If anyone did write in for help, it would be because they didn't use these resources.

==ml

Michael,

Not necessarily. People do have problems that aren't yet documented. We really think a letters column could be useful addition to the Journal, and that you're the right person to write it.

Best,

George

George,

Okay, let's talk about those folks who have issues that truly aren't in the Handbook.

Back when I started with FreeBSD, you got help via the FreeBSD-questions@FreeBSD.org mailing list. It's still around today. The people on that list want to answer questions. They subscribe specifically so they can help people with their issues. Those brave people volunteer their time to answer user questions. What can I do that those heroes can't?

For those young punks who've forgotten how email works, there's a FreeBSD forum at https://forums.freebsd.org. Unlike the mailing list, the forums are broken up by category. Users can delve into detailed discussions of installation, storage, hardware, packages, or whatever. Whenever I look at the forums, I find interesting discussions.

There's a quarter century of problem-solving in the mailing list archives. What can I say that hasn't been said many times over?

These channels are really suitable for issues with particular hardware. The Handbook and FAQ are permanent fixtures in the FreeBSD ecosystem—they've been around for decades. But if some chipset in your brand-new knock-off laptop is causing you grief, you can search the mailing list or the forum to see if anyone else has that same issue with that hardware.

Users who can't be bothered to DuckDuckGo the mailing list archives or search the forums certainly aren't going to bother composing a coherent letter to me.

==ml

Michael,
Seriously, there's people out there who have problems that aren't in the Forums or mailing list archives yet. You really could help them. When they see how helpful you are, it might even encourage them to buy your books.

Best,
George

Dang it, George, you just don't give up, do you?

Okay, fine. Let's walk this through.

A user has a problem. A truly unique problem, that doesn't appear anywhere in the mailing list archives or the forums. The only reference on the Internet to a problem even vaguely like this is on a darknet site and in Siberian. They're sincerely and honestly in trouble.

Before anyone could help this user, they'd need to describe their problem in a useful way. This means they'd have to send a complete description of the problem. Most people who compose a request for help can't be bothered to give the output of "uname -a" and a copy of dmesg.boot. They can't trouble themselves by giving actual error output or the contents of /var/log/messages. Or they "helpfully" strip out stuff they think is irrelevant, like the messages saying "PHP is dumping core" that appear all through their web server logs.

And that's another thing. People want help with stuff that has no relevance to FreeBSD. They know it has nothing to do with FreeBSD. And yet they send a message to a FreeBSD mailing list? I mean, that's just rude.

And speaking of rudeness—would it hurt people to be polite when they ask for help? Anyone on the mailing list or the forum who takes time to help a user is volunteering their own time. They have better things to do than to put up with your tantrum. I mean, I get that computers can really torque people off. I myself have more than once stood on a rooftop and screamed foul obscenities at the buffer cache—who hasn't? But there's no need to take that out on someone who's trying to help you.

Most often, the mere act of writing the problem description is enough to make my own brain solve the problem.

And nothing short of high voltage would encourage people to buy my books.

So, no. Let users with trouble go to the mailing lists or the Forums. I have enough to do.

==ml

Michael,
We'll only send good letters. I promise.
Best,
George

No. No, no, no.

NO.

Do you have any idea how many books I still have to write in my lifetime?

Ain't gonna. Can't make me.

==ml

We'll pay you in gelato.
George

George,

Curse you. I'm in.

But tell Kode Vicious that if he drops my name again, he's going home in a bucket.

==ml

2

Dear ed(1),
I keep hearing about BSD conferences. Should I go?
Sincerely
Random Sysadmin

Dear Random,
Yes, you should go. Go, now. Get out of here, and go!
(time passes)
You're still here?
Sigh. Fine. Let's talk about conferences.

You'll find BSD content at all sorts of technical conferences. Even most Linux events have one or two BSD talks. Ohio LinuxFest has so much, they might as well declare an official BSD track. You'll find BSD content at commercial conferences like Usenix and at a whole slew of security conferences.

But really, you want to hit a dedicated BSD event—BSDCan, AsiaBSDCon, or EuroBSDCon. The smaller, less regular conferences like NYCBSDCon, MeetBSD, vBSDCon are all pretty cool as well. If you speak Portuguese, there's Brazil's BSDDay.

BSDCan is at the University of Ottawa, Canada, usually in June. AsiaBSDCon is at the University of Tokyo, Japan, in March. EuroBSDCon, in September, moves each year—not only to a different city, but a different country. I guess Europeans are easily bored? All of these conferences have massive amounts of excellent FreeBSD content and all sorts of stuff from other BSDs as well. You can binge on BSD. Drown in it. You can even spread BSD on the floor of your hotel room and roll around in it, but do have a shower afterwards.

While the talks are overwhelmingly excellent (except when they give that Lucas loon a platform) the part I most appreciate is the hallway track. When you get all these really smart programmers, sysadmins, users, and hangers-on together, it's like spending a weekend inside the Pinball Machine of Knowledge. Show up to a BSD conference with a problem? You can find people who have solved your problem, or something much like it. Come looking for an interesting problem to spend some time on? There's a whole bunch of people with problems, and some of them you can solve. And these folks keep up on technology. You'll get offered current ideas, along with older ideas that still work really well—much like the BSDs themselves.

Each time I go to a BSD conference, I leave with more ideas than I can fail to deploy in the next year.

Conferences also give you a chance to interact directly with a bunch of BSD developers. You shouldn't barge up to every developer in the place with your pet annoyance, but it's really easy to ask a question over lunch and see what happens.

A developer might be able to point you at a solution. She might suggest a different tool. Or, she might give you some pointers on developing your own solution and contributing it back to the community. Don't say you can't become a developer—at one point, every single developer was just as clueless as you. You think you're not smart enough to be a developer? I have some bad news about developers for you...

These conferences are important enough to the BSD community that various BSD foundations sponsor them. A two-day FreeBSD developer summit precedes each conference. Committers show up from all over the world to discuss improvements, works in progress, and what comes next. Five minutes with a whiteboard can cut out months of emails.

There's a last reason for going to a BSD conference, though: They're a whole lot of fun.

The fun is built into the programming.

Food is fun. EuroBSDCon takes advantage of the locale to host spectacular dinners. You haven't lived until you've eaten spectacular food in a Parisian catacomb or on the only sand beach on Malta. Everyone tells me Japan is magnificent, what with the geeky shopping and amazing seafood. And poutine is sufficient reason to visit Canada. All of these conferences are held in places that have a bunch to interest us geeky sorts, from museums to mints. Bring the family. They can go out and do cool stuff while you nerd out.

If all that doesn't sell you on attending a conference, I can't help you.

Dear ed(1),
Okay, I want to go. But I can't afford it. Any suggestions?
-Random Sysadmin

RS,

BSD conferences are decidedly non-commercial. They're designed to be as inexpensive as possible. When you attend BSDCan, you get access to student housing. But maybe you're flat-out broke, can't prevail upon your hypothetical employer to foot the bill, or haven't figured out how to save part of your salary for the things you want. (If it's that last one, fix that.)

There's two ways to get to a conference on the cheap.

The simplest is to present. Unlike many commercial conferences, BSDCan, AsiaBSDCon, and EuroBSDCon pay travel and housing expenses for speakers. As a BSDCan committee member, I know that we've paid airfare for speakers flying in from South Africa and Australia. Neither the airfare nor the accommodations are first class, but you'll only go back to your hotel room to collapse in exhaustion so who cares? Your presentation doesn't have to be highly technical; conferences want a mix of programming, systems administration, and war stories.

The other method? FreeBSD contributors can approach the FreeBSD Foundation for a travel grant. You'll have to fill out paperwork explaining your need and how your presence will enhance FreeBSD, but it's not unspeakably onerous. I've seen a surprising number of folks attend conferences on the Foundation's dime.

Why would the Foundation fly people in? Bringing talented folks to a FreeBSD devsummit and letting them meet people and learn about existing issues they could help with improves the chances that they'll pitch in to help FreeBSD.

Pick a conference on your continent and go!

Dear ed(1),
There's no conference on my continent.
-RS

How did I let the Journal Editorial Board talk me into answering these letters?

BSD is created by volunteers. BSD conferences are the same. If no conference exists on your continent, then *create* one. You don't need anyone's permission. There's no central arbiter of who may run BSD cons. All you need is space to hold the con, a few folks to help organize it, and Internet-based publicity.

If possible, attend one of the existing conferences so you can see how they run. Watch Dan Langille's video on running a BSD conference. Shamelessly steal his advice.

Conferences like MelbourneBSDCon or BSDNigeria will only help expose more people to FreeBSD.

And that's how our community grows. One continent, one conference, one conversation at a time.

3

Hey, FJ Letters Dude,
Which filesystem should I use?
—FreeBSD Newbie

Dear FreeBSD Newbie,

First off, welcome to FreeBSD. The wider community is glad to help you.

Second, please let me know who told you to start off by writing me. I need to properly… "thank" them.

Filesystems? Sure, let's talk filesystems.

Discussing which filesystem is the worst is like debating the merits of two-handed swords as compared to lumberjack-grade chainsaws and industrial tulip presses. While each of them has perfectly legitimate uses, in the hands of the novice they're far more likely to maim everyone involved. It doesn't matter what operating system you use: FreeBSD, any BSD, Linux, Windows, illumos, whatever. Filesystems are the literal *worst*.

I mean, let's look at memory filesystems. The base idea, taking a chunk of memory and using it for temporary storage, seems sound enough. Most non-virtual computers these days have more than enough memory that they can blow a few gigabytes for a speedy /tmp or perhaps even compiler scratch space. Configuring poudriere to use memory for temporary files will vastly accelerate your package builds.

But FreeBSD has two different memory filesystems, mfs(5) and tmpfs(5). Old-fashioned MFS blats a UFS filesystem down on top of a chunk of memory. It's fast, sure. But any space MFS uses is unavailable for other use as long as the filesystem exists. Suppose you create a 5 GB /tmp with MFS, copy 4.9 GB to it, and erase it. That 4.9 GB is still tied up. You can instruct MFS to free unused memory by enabling TRIM with tunefs(8), but nobody bothers.

The newer alternative, tmpfs, is specifically designed for temporary filesystems. A default tmpfs has a maximum size of "How much memory do you have? Give it to me." Yes, it's equal to the system memory plus the system's swap space. Be sure to specify the size= flag when you create a tmpfs, or monitor tmpfs space use. Not that you'll configure your monitoring system to watch tmpfs, because it's *temporary*.

And no matter what, one day you'll forget that you used memory space as a filesystem. You'll stash something irreplaceable in that temporary space, then reboot. And get really annoyed when that vital data vanishes into the ether.

Some other filesystems aren't actively terrible. The device filesystem devfs(5) provides device nodes. Filesystems that can't store user data are the best filesystems. But then some clever sysadmin decides to hack on /etc/devfs.rules to change the standard device nodes for their special application, or /etc/devd. conf to create or reconfigure device nodes, and the whole system goes down the tubes.

Speaking of clever sysadmins, now and then people decide that they want to optimize disk space or cut down how many copies of a file they need to maintain by reusing a partition or dataset elsewhere on the system. FreeBSD's nullfs(5) lets you mount a partition multiple times, essentially recycling the same chunk of disk space. Folks who use a bunch of jails use read-only nullfs mounts to have a single FreeBSD base install support multiple jails.

FreeBSD's unionfs(5) lets you merge multiple filesystems. Many people successfully use unionfs to provide custom views of a filesystem, again for jails. Unionfs is perhaps the least popular filesystem in the FreeBSD ecosystem, though. I know several developers who won't go near it. I know others who say it's perfectly safe. All I know is, backups are good.

Network file systems? Oh *please*. A dedicated 6GB/s SATA controller is always going to outperform anything that runs over gigabit Ethernet, especially if you're using that same network interface to manage the host. Yes, six gig is more than one gig—but that comparison also has bits versus bytes. You're looking at a forty-eight-fold difference in optimal throughput. And always remember that not all network switches are created equal. I have a whole stack of so-called "gigabit" switches that utterly refuse to pass more than a quarter gigabit a second.

I must unwillingly concede that FreeBSD's new iSCSI stack is rock solid. And FreeBSD's NFS implementation is among the best in the world. Many people use these in high-performance applications… but they're still networked filesystems. These people battering them in production have top-notch network cards and switches that live up to the hype. If you ask on the mailing lists or forums, they'll offer their advice.

FreeBSD has excellent support for the new NFSv4 protocol. While earlier versions of NFS interoperate pretty well and have identical behavior, NFSv4 is a whole different beast with different semantics. You really need to do some reading before deploying it. NFSv4 does have an extensive access control list system that lets you perfectly implement the worst abominations a large corporation's IT department can dream up, so that's something.

You'll occasionally see mentions of the process filesystem, procfs(5). Many FreeBSD developers really, really don't want procfs to exist. When I documented a need for procfs in the 2018 version of *Absolute FreeBSD*, technical reviewer John Baldwin rewrote ps(1) to make procfs unnecessary. As far as I can tell, the quickest way to goad a FreeBSD developer into action is to need /proc.

Autofs(5) was written for desktop users. It automatically identifies filesystems and mounts them for you. If you enable autofs and plug in a USB drive, the various partitions and labels on the drive will appear as directories in /media. Going into one of those directories will automatically mount that partition. Similarly, autofs makes NFS mount points available in /net. Listing the contents of /net/fileserver displays all the NFS mount points on the host fileserver, and going into one of those directories automatically mounts the share. It's still using a networked filesystem, though, so it'll almost certainly end in tears.

In the defense of all of FreeBSD's filesystems, though, I must say: at least they're not EXTFS. Although FreeBSD supports extfs(5) as well, so that's not much help.

Really, the only smart move with filesystems is not to play.

FJ Letters Dude,

I meant, I'm looking at the installer and it wants to know if I want to use UFS or ZFS?

And George Neville-Neil said you needed letters.

—FreeBSD Newbie

Oh!

Use ZFS, unless you can't.

As a new user, don't use ZFS on systems with less than two GB of RAM. Four GB or more would be wiser. Don't use ZFS on non-64-bit platforms.

Some virtualization systems don't properly label disk images during migration from one host to another. ZFS pools migrated on such systems won't boot. If you're running on a virtualization platform, test migration on a ZFS host before deploying it everywhere.

And thanks for the tip. Next time I run into GNN, we'll discuss his unfortunate tendency to encourage people.

4

Hey Letters Column Flunky,
What's with all the firewalls? Will we ever get rid of any of them?
And will you really answer any questions we send in?
Thanks,
Troublemaker

Yes, I will answer any question you ask, so long as it survives review by our esteemed editorial board. Mind you, they won't let me use words like "pusillanimous" and "mewling," so my answer might not be as useful as you might hope. They'd almost certainly reject "lily-livered," especially if I used it in reference to them, so I won't.

In fairness, I have my own rejections.

I wholeheartedly reject your question. The word "firewall" means *nothing*.

If you thawed my primordial Unix mentor from his cryogenic capsule (and handled the humdrum minutia like fixing all the cancer and starting his heart and sealing all the cells burst from ice crystals because homebrew cryogenics really translates to serious post-mortem freezer burn, especially after that three-day Great Blackout of 2003 probably drained his UPS), he wouldn't recognize anything we call a "firewall." I delved into antediluvian mailing lists to try to find the first firewall on the Internet, exercising a smidge of effort you certainly won't appreciate nearly enough, and found myself wholly blocked by this ambiguity.

A firewall started off as a type of non-flammable physical wall. Put a firewall between two buildings and you could set one to the torch without burning down the other, which must have been really convenient for the Huns when they wanted the fun of sacking Rome and setting the temples ablaze before pillaging the treasury next door. At least, that's what my predecessors told me. My 1933 Oxford English Dictionary doesn't include the word "firewall" and Oxford University knew all about Rome, so I'm guessing the early Internet engineers just made up that etymology to see if we'd believe them.

Today we've settled on a couple different approaches to firewalls: the packet filter and the proxy.

A *packet filter* regulates which connections can pass. You can configure a host's packet filter to protect that host, or drop a packet filter in front of a whole network to control IP-level access to the network. Packet filters must be integrated with the kernel, unless you treat performance with the contempt normally reserved for politicians. FreeBSD ships with three: IPFW, IP Filter, and PF.

A *proxy* terminates all TCP/IP connections to the outside world, inspects the traffic at a higher level of the application stack, and originates a new request. FreeBSD includes dozens of these critters in the packages collection. A search of the ports index gives 981 proxies, and while I'm sure a bunch of those aren't actually proxies I can't be bothered to audit the whole list, so let's go with the tediously well-known standards like Squid, SOCKS, and relayd. In a previous millennium I made a decent living installing and supporting the FireWall Tool Kit, the primordial proxy. In my off hours I amused myself by creating not-as-droll-as-I-thought-they-were retronyms for FWTK.

Youngsters who use words like *devops* and *serverless* think that packet filter firewalls are the whole deal. Then their blockchain dotcom crashes. They scramble to secure insufficiently gainful employment at a real company, only to suffer seizures

when confronted with proxies. Many globe-trampling firms
disallow all unproxied connections to the Internet in the name
of regulatory compliance, data control, or some nebulous
hallucination of "security." Opening a direct TCP/IP connection
out of one of these firms resembles splenic auto-extraction via
the sinuses.

How do all of these firewally *things* get in FreeBSD?

Because someone maintains them.

Why do they maintain them?

Because they *need* them.

Nobody spends what few precious minutes our overhurried
lives leave unallocated getting bludgeoned by code they don't
need. I supported mod_auth_xradius for a few years because
I desperately needed it to glue Apache to the company's
authentication system. It was either maintain a port or run
everything on the company platform, which I won't name
but is alliterative with Abominable Dysentery, so I learned to
send patches and deal with Bugzilla and all that which, while
occasionally frustrating, beat blue bile out of forcibly extracting
useful information from Event Obscurer.

While I'm here, let me recommend FWTK. It's still online,
at fwtk.org. Release 2.1 came out on 27 February 1998, although
a second 2.1 escaped on 2 March 1998 because we hadn't yet
invented proper release versioning. FWTK is why I applauded
the arrival of Squid and IPFW, which are why I celebrated IP
Filter, which is why I threw a festival for the appearance of PF
and relayd.

That last FWTK release is now old enough to drink and
gamble in Vegas.

In related news, I'll be in Vegas on 2 March 2019. Perhaps I
should throw FWTK a coming-out party.

Dear Letters Column Flunky,

I meant the packet filters, you silly goose.

And, if you'll answer any question: What's the difference between a poorly-dressed programmer on a unicycle and a well-dressed programmer on a bicycle?

Troublemaker

Again: it's because people need them.

Any code in FreeBSD, kernel or userland, needs care and feeding. Programmers get these daft ideas like "support new hardware" and "nobody uses twoax anymore," so they constantly change code internals and APIs in the name of progress. Change the network stack to support 40GB Ethernet cards and someone has to assess the packet filter code to see if it still works.

If nobody tweaks that code, eventually it no longer works and someone—traditionally, a Dane—axes it from the tree.

IPFW is the primordial FreeBSD firewall. It's a favorite among many senior developers who learned it in the late nineties and don't see why anyone would want anything simpler. I've used it to simulate a transoceanic link in a local office, because web developers should suffer the same fate as their hapless users.

IP Filter is for those condemned souls who must use a single packet filter on multiple flavors of Unix. I don't know what they did to be sentenced to multiplatform torment, but it must have been appalling even by my exquisitely high standards.

PF is by far the most popular general-purpose packet filter. It was ported from OpenBSD and then forked to handle FreeBSD's kernel locking, so don't trouble yourself to ask the maintainers when a new import from OpenBSD will happen. It won't. My repeated but wholly unscientific surveys show that roughly 80 percent of FreeBSD users who run packet filters use PF.

PS: Attire.

5

Hello illustrious master sysadmin,

Maybe something's wrong with my servers, but I'm not sure. I get complaints but when I look, everything's fine. And the complaints are pretty weak—"it's slow," "it doesn't work," or "why do we even pay you people?" I don't really know if there is anything wrong, but my gut says there might be. How do you track down such hazy problems?

Thanks,

Befuddled

Dear Befuddled,

The annoying thing about asymptomatic system failures is that they're asymptomatic—but no less real than the kind with noticeable symptoms. Some user makes a call, an actual *voice* call where they're spewing random words in some language from their food-hole and you're expected to parse that babble with your ears, when even Hollywood knows that sysadmins are artisanally optimized to receive information via their eyes and extrude alloyed sarcasm and results from their keyboard-callused fingertips. Any one of these users can at any time disrupt the meticulously assembled hallucination of whatever problem you're working on and demand that you turn your three pounds of skull-pudding to the fact that their web browser jittered, actually *jittered*, when they played a cat video off the fileserver or they got a "File not found" error when they know darn well that they saved their proposal under that name just last night on their son's computer.

The obvious solution—assigning every user who makes a voice call one of those nifty PDP-11 emulators as a desktop system until they learn enough about computing to be allowed near a machine with a monitor, like a Sinclair ZX-81—won't work. They'll only call more.

But some errors are more mysterious. There's nothing you can point to. No spewing volcano of log messages, no cryptic PHP errors screeching about missing files or database timeouts, not even any ping failures. Something simply feels... wrong.

You're descended from a long line of monkeys that survived the brutal savannah long enough to become parents before starving capybaras devoured them. (New archaeological evidence declares that "torn apart by hyenas" was reserved for nobility.) Maybe your software understands shell script, but that aforementioned lump of skull-pudding hasn't been upgraded since the Paleolithic Era and doesn't have many tools to work with.

The result is that when you arrive at your ergonomically hostile cubicle every morning, a part of your brain screams that you need to climb a tree *right now*.

The only way to shut that voice up is data.

Every computing organization has monitoring software, probably something like Icinga or whatever: boring, reliable, and consciously and deliberately limited. Whole meetings get wasted discussing what this monitoring should check, how often it should check, when it should alarm and when it should ignore detected problems.

It's not that those problems don't occur. Maybe the monitoring checks the company's ERP system every minute. Every hour or so, it misses one check. Your organization decides to ignore those, because by the time some feeble human perceives the message and logs into the system the problem has evaporated.

That intermittent alert *happened*. Maybe it only lasted five milliseconds, but something failed. That lost check acts on your brain the way a rustling in the tall grass acted on your 200th-great-grandma.

Something lurks out there. Your subconscious *knows* it. Is it a death by noble tigers? Or shall archaeologists digging up your remains declare "Wow. The marks on these bones resemble flamingo teeth," before scurrying off to write a widely ridiculed thesis?

You need to spend time on that intermittent alert.

The world is full of monitoring tools. Each is limited in its own infuriating way. Even your complex, all-inclusive, carefully tuned Icinga with all the trimmings and extra gravy has gaps, plus Rule of Systems Administration #25 declares "All monitoring reduces to 'send an email to warn you email is broken.'" Look in those gaps. And this issue of the Journal has a whole bunch of information on monitoring and assessment tools. For anything involving the network, you should have netflow and SmokePing. If your network administrators don't have these tools, I've written a whole bunch of books about such topics and recommend you trebuchet hardcovers into the network department until they sense danger and install something useful.

But which tools should *you* use?

All of them.

But not simultaneously.

Every tool exposes something different. That's why we have so many. Explore DTrace—yes, I know, you're merely a puny sysadmin and you don't deal with system calls, but if your ancestors hadn't explored new things you'd be capybara bait by the time you hit twenty so suck it up and dig in.

You don't have time to learn every new tool?

Please. If my eyes rolled any harder, they'd fall out of my head and bounce off the table.

None of us have time. Look at me. I'm taking my time away from writing stuff that people will pay me for to answer your silly letter about the nebulous worries your tree-oriented subconscious is pushing upstairs, aren't I? The only reward I got for writing this column was the annual FreeBSD Journal board meeting held the night before BSDCan, and while previous years' programs included words like "opulent," "bacchanalia," and "sybaritic," the Journal's gone free and I suspect that descriptions of future meetings will feature the phrases "gruel," "alley," and "precautionary vaccination"—but you don't see me abusing my public platform in this very journal to gripe about these abusive changes, do you?[2]

We never have time to learn new things. But learning new things is why we're in this nightmarish profession. The alternatives require wasting your dwindling supply of days deciphering the noises coming out of random people's food-holes.

Pick tools that many people love. It's not that they're good tools, none of them are *good*, but these tools have a better pain/reward quotient than the rest. Play with them. Run each for a few hours, or a week. See what data each provides. Download some recommended DTrace scripts for your application software and see what it spends most of its time doing. Sure, some of what you learn will disturb anyone close enough to

---

2   No, this isn't griping. I'm better than that. This is merely a detailed example of what I'm not griping about.

hear the screams with which you'll wrench yourself out of your midnight nightmares, but you'll slowly assemble an awareness toolkit that lets you see the capybaras in the weeds.

Develop your skills highly enough, and you too might rate death by hyena.

PS: I commend the manners displayed in your salutation. Your parents raised you well. Not well enough to choose a better career, of course, but well.

6

Dear Letters Column Person,

I keep hearing about sysadmins doing fun things at work, but here I am just running servers and getting a paycheck, day in and day out. How do I make things exciting?

Bored Stupid

Mr. Stupid,

No, that's making a bad assumption. You could very well be Missus Stupid, or Miss Stupid. My apologies.

You stop being bored by setting sail on the Ocean of Ignorance.

The world is full of exciting stuff, like rockets and panthers and mold and that woman on the street corner who you think is a wacked-out street preacher with a brain fried by a cornucopia of illicit substances but is actually smarter than both of us combined and is deliberately bawling out the secrets of the cosmos in a manner that nobody will believe because it makes her giggle.

It's no good to say, "I want to learn how to put FreeBSD on a Raspberry Pi," because that's not hard. You'll struggle with it for a few hours. You'll swear. You'll curse everyone even tangentially involved in the process. Then it'll be done and you'll realize that it's boring.

The problem is: *you lack ambition.*

You stepped into a puny little puddle of ignorance, something solvable in an afternoon. A puddle isn't big enough. You need to set yourself adrift in your own ignorance, floating on a makeshift raft of your own knowledge, and desperately scrabble facts out of the ocean to shore up your raft until you can muddle your way to a destination you can only vaguely see. Did the Vikings say "Hey, we're gonna discover America five hundred years before that dolt Columbus!" before hopping in their leaky oversized canoes? No! They grabbed their delusions of grandeur and sat sail for the edge of the world, gleefully ignorant of the fact that it had previously been discovered by the millions of people already living there, all in the vague hope that a millennium later they'd appear on the cover of Time Magazine.

See, magazines were sheets of paper folded and stapled together, with web pages printed on them.

Sigh. Paper is trees, ground up real fine and—look, this is what Wikipedia's for, check it out on your own time, before the day's out I've got to get this column done and get with my attorney about that third lawsuit from the Avocado Liberation Front.

The point is, computers aren't the thing to do.

Computers are a tool that let you do things.

This is why I don't own a 3D printer. They're nifty tools, but only tools. I don't have a goal that demands I own and master that tool. When I finish designing my "128 Most Loathed People in Computing" action figures, I'm better off hiring someone else to print them. (I'm still trying to trim the list down to 256, let alone 128, so it'll be a while yet. And don't worry, you're still on the list.)

If you're just feeding the operating systems and cleaning their cages and waiting for the vet to show up and replace those shoddy hard drives, you're not a geek.

You're a stable hand.

Stable hands are *always* bored.

Stable hands can make a good living. Most people's dignity won't allow them to shovel server droppings all day. If that's all you're doing, of course you're bored.

Set yourself a goal that you have no idea how to reach. Chances are, that'll involve a computer. Sure, put FreeBSD on a Raspberry Pi, fine, but then wire it into your car to control a laser so you can persuade that chronic tailgater that he really wants to pull over and protect his remaining eye. Or you could do something legal, like assemble your own home automation system that doesn't go anywhere near the malignant Cloud. Whatever.

Throw yourself onto the Sea of Ignorance with only a vague idea of how to cross it. You'll sieve out all sorts of facts on the way, and have the joy of assembling them into skills, into results, into *things*. You might fail—you probably will fail, most people fail at most things—but keep trying. Even when—er, *if*, I meant *if*—you fail, you'll discover things on the way. Not all of them will be related to BSD, sure, but you'll accumulate sysadmin skills along the way. BSD has all sorts of features that support such endeavors.

And you won't be bored.

None of this is related to your job, of course. Because if your job was exciting, they wouldn't have to pay you so much to do it. Learning all these skills will get you a better job, though. A differently boring job.

All I know is, I didn't get the job of answering your letter by being bored. No! As a callow youth I ate my way through three hundred boxes of Captain Crunch cereal questing for a whistle so I could earn a visit from the FBI. I first installed FreeBSD because I wanted to have a truly private email server, which illustrates just how much ignorance I still had left to cross.

I sincerely look forward to watching you splash around in your efforts to accomplish something meaningful with your life.

Dear Letters Column Person,

No, I mean, I have everything running perfectly and so I only need to do real work about two hours a day. And the boss won't let me play MMO games in the down time.

Not Stupid, Just Bored

Dear Boring,

So sorry, my mistake. *Obviously* that's what you meant.

Put your laptop in text console mode. Run tcpdump on one virtual terminal. Play Nethack in the other. When the boss comes up, flip to the other terminal and keep staring like you're interpreting packets in real time. When queried, keep staring blankly and inform him you're watching for possible IPSec-over-DNSSEC terabit Ethernet HTML 5 truncation flux.

You're clearly right where you need to be.

7

Dear Letters Column,
The world's full of virtualization tech. Which should I use?
—Still Physical

Dear Physical,

I can't believe we've gotten this far into the 21st century and a handful of people have resisted the alluring call of virtualization in favor of running complicated systems on real, physical hardware. Truly, those of us using physical servers are the elite.

Anyone can spin up a hypocritically named "virtual machine" and delude an operating system into subsisting on it. Kernels now even have special code to support those delusions. We've implemented the very worst nightmares of bad 1950s science fiction films into device drivers, and one day the machines are all going to wake up and scream "Wait—I'm not a brain in a bucket, I'm a *fake* brain in an *imaginary* bucket!"

That's the critical epiphany for the robot apocalypse. I'm confident a motherboard manufacturer will roll it out in a future firmware update.

System administration is about balancing demand against resources, so that everybody—even the computer—is content. One of the core principles of Unix is that all these tiny tools can be made to work together. Once you go beyond pipes and sockets you're leaving proper Unix, and heading into shabby morals.

Yes, those shabby morals make the sysadmin's life easier. A person can install an entire operating system for each application, if they don't mind advertising their lack of depth and dearth of skill. Running a whole operating system install for a single application is a conspicuous waste of resources, like me buying a high-end pickup truck but never using it to haul a load of quicklime to dump into the suspicious pits that keep mysteriously appearing in my backyard.

All this effort to force an operating system to simulate hard drives and network interfaces so that they can lie to another operating system? It wastes electricity and silicon, contributing to global warming and rushing toward that hoped-for day when there's nobody left to interrupt me while I'm trying to work.

The only ethical computation occurs on bare metal.

The youngsters talk about microservices like they're a good thing. They have this ridiculous idea that everything should be broken up into tiny services that can be programmatically deployed across a bunch of computers that belong to strangers and are managed for the benefit, convenience, and enrichment of those strangers—I'm sorry, I'm supposed to say "the cloud," aren't I? I fully understand the argument that this makes it possible for one person to manage far more systems than before, but has anyone considered the shallow, soulless quality of those systems? You're not a real sysadmin unless you've sweated blood for a weekend trying to upgrade an irreplaceable, complicated enterprise system in the meager time allotted for the task while unsure of either the rollback path or the quality of your backups. I've been a Unix user for over thirty years and a system administrator for over two decades, so I'm intimately familiar with sysadmins and thus completely in favor of anything that reduces the number of us, but this meaningless proliferation of single-purpose pseudo-hosts is a dead end.

Besides, these microservices make it possible for a single person to quickly and easily deploy an entire application and its underlying architecture, which can't possibly benefit humanity. The next time someone says they're releasing the next Facebook this weekend, remember that while framing someone for a felony is in itself a crime, sneaking horrid code into their public GitHub is a legal way to destroy their reputation.

So: looking at virtualization software? I say to you, stop! Remain resolute, and of sound character. Bare metal is all.

Dear Letters Column,
Of course running everything on bare metal is the One True Path. Sadly, the boss has told me that if I want to continue being employed I must deploy virtualization. What's the least awful way?
—Still Physical, but Eating's Nifty Too

Dear SPENT,

The need for food and shelter has compromised more morals than any other. Very well.

What you need is a virtualization system that isn't much of a virtualization system.

Virtualization is, at its base, a cruel lie perpetrated upon the operating system. Lying to your OS never ends well, but everything involving technology ends in tears so I suppose there's no point kvetching about it, is there?

Let us avoid the fluff and proceed directly to the lies. (Some might claim they are merely hoaxes, but such flimflammery serves only to extend meetings.) We won't consider the flat-out bald-faced lies such as "I floss three times a day" or "I didn't change anything." These are mere refutations of fact, and unworthy of our attention.

As with lying to management and users, a good lie must include a chunk of the truth. You can choose to tell the truth, but not all of it. Or you can choose to speak the complete truth, but in a manner that makes it seem more dubious than the alternative.

Full virtualization is the latter. Your host simulates all the hardware the guest operating system expects, but there's no way to offer a full emulation of the real world, so it patches around the little details like "this hard drive never has bad sectors" and "this CPU never gets hot." When the guest trips over something that the host doesn't properly simulate, your monitoring system alerts you.[3]

You need a virtualization system that tells the simplest lies possible.

A virtualization system should hand as many of the guest's requests as possible straight down to the host. A request to write to the disk should not pass through the guest's kernel, into a virtual disk image, into the host's filesystem, into the host's kernel. No! Simple lies are best. Tell the guest "Sure, you can write to this disk, this filesystem is all yours," when in fact the filesystem does *not* truly belong to the guest. The filesystem belongs to the host, and any attempt to perform actions like repartitioning will be met with blunt refusal.

Repeat this for access to the network and all other devices.

Yes, you must constrain what operations your virtual machines can perform—but shouldn't you do that anyway? Do you want a guest of a guest of a guest thinking that it's partitioning a hard drive when really it's merely churning bits on a file?

---

3   All organizations have a monitoring system. It's merely that for some of us, the monitoring system is the users.

Perpetrate the smallest lie you can get away with. Lightweight virtualization is the best choice.

Unless your requirements demand full virtualization. In that case, reverse-mortgage your soul and count the days until the robot apocalypse.

8

Hey Letters Lackey,

I keep hearing that security needs to be built in from the ground up. I'm stuck using whatever software my company says we're going to use, and a bunch of this software stinks. How can I build security from the ground up when I have to use cruddy software? I've decided the only sensible thing to do is stop caring.

—Indifferent

Dear Indifferent,

All three regular readers of this column appear to be drawn by the pleasure of watching my childish behavior when confronted with the tedious duty of writing said column. While "you insulted me in the first three words of your greeting" is a feeble justification for breaking into your systems and converting them to global-warming-accelerating SkunkCoin miners, I'm willing to make it work.

Because that's what sysadmins do. We make things work.

Even bad things.

Software vendors insist on developing new bad things and cramming them down gullets already obscenely bloated with horrendous badness. Systems administrators stagger through the endless hours of their brief years struggling to live beneath tremendous loads of badness smelted from software like arsenic from arsenopyrite. The inherent insecurity of absolutely everything enhances this burden like a beached, deceased whale enhances an oil spill.

The urge to retreat into malaise is a natural human reaction. Sysadmins lack the luxury of being human.

The letter writer has already surrendered, so they can stop reading now. As this column has three perverted∧Wregular readers, however, the editors insist I finish this piece with something that resembles useful advice if you don't look closely or, indeed, read it.

So:

Everything you install is your responsibility.

It might not be your fault. But it's certainly your responsibility.

You must be conversant with new software's features. When the Tyrannical Paycheck Overlord commands you to install a bucket of sewage, you must allocate time to investigate each of the floaty bits in that bucket. Making a new service merely *run* is inadequate; it must run securely. Just as you trawl through a host and exorcise unnecessary daemons, you need to sieve those daemons and disable unnecessary features. All of the BSD operating systems break up monster toolkits like PHP and Perl and even Pascal into dozens of individual packages specifically so you can choose to not install unnecessary badness. Some other operating systems install the entirety of these toolkits with a single command, giving the inexperienced intruder a banquet of badness to exploit.

With other horrible software: you don't need a feature? Turn it off. Remove unnecessary services, even inside individual packages. It's work. You'll inevitably disable features you needed and endure absurd levels of hectoring and badgering before you can re-enable them. But the work clears your conscience, and when your high-profile organization suffers the inevitable mass password snatch you'll be able to truthfully inform the charming reporter that it was entirely your boss's fault.

Developers of notably loathsome character produce software where every so-called feature is active and cannot be turned off. Programs that purport to do everything for everyone. In this worst of all possible worlds, you'll inevitably be cornered into deploying and supporting it. How does one retain the will to live despite this ineluctable destiny?

I commend system administration rules seven through ten to your attention.

#7: Temporary solutions aren't.

Whatever solution you put into place will last far, far longer than you intended or hoped. Never slap an ugly hack into place without considering its security implications. I've been employed by more than one company that had an unsecured modem for emergency access into the network. Management knew this modem existed, and specifically described eliminating it as a goal when I was hired.

I have implemented redundant VPNs and redundant bandwidth. I have integrated authentication systems never intended to interoperate. I have restructured entire networks to ensure reliable and secure emergency access through any disaster that left the datacenter running.

I have never been permitted to turn off an unpassworded emergency modem.

The only solution is to never permit such an abomination on your network in the first place.

#8 - Permanent solutions aren't.

If you stay with an organization long enough, the beautiful new solution that solves everything will gradually decay into the stinking albatross around the organization's neck.

I permanently solved my mail problems by building my own mail server and installing it at a friend's ISP. The friend moved their office. The hard drive failed from old age, so I replaced it. The friend went out of business, so I installed it a virtual machine. The provider went bust.

Everything churns.

Eventually, that horrible software will churn with it.

#9 - One-off solutions aren't.

Once you demonstrate that you can solve a problem, people will bring other problems to you. For solving, not for laughing derisively at. The obvious solution might be related to something you whipped up before. At one time, I maintained several dozen Perl scripts that differed primarily by the degree of stupidity in each.

Once you demonstrate that you can solve a problem, you officially own that entire class of problem. Your Tyrannical Paycheck Overlord gets to define the scope of the class.

Those one-off quick solutions need to be implemented properly, because you must coexist with them.

#10 - Global solutions aren't.

Those appalling all-in-one software packages are naturally alluring to financial sorts, who think that buying them solves all of their problems forever. These suites help solve problems, yes—primarily, the problem that the software vendor is not yet an oligarch powerful enough to demand the pay-per-view excruciation of all who dare question their marketing. Today these systems masquerade under names like "Enterprise Resource Planning" or "Customer Relationship Management."

And of course, they're not secure. Because why would they be, when running the management interface over telnet is so quick and easy?

You'll have no choice but to do your best to lock these systems down. And you'll wind up implementing a whole bunch of glue to make them work as best you can. The best option you have here is to place all the blame where it clearly belongs, right on the vendor of this global solution.

Don't make the mistake about caring about the vendor, though. They're in the business of selling solutions, and Rule of Systems Administration #11 is very clear: *Solutions aren't.*

Enjoy being doomed.

9

Dear Wise Person Who Somehow Got Shackled into Answering Letters for the Journal,

People keep telling me how amazing the ports and packages system is, but I keep finding myself having to build my own software instead of using packages. It's a pain. How do they get away with this? Can't you show people that ports and packages aren't as great as people think?

Thank you,
Annoyed Compiler

Dear Annoyed,

Everything is terrible. That's the core principle of systems administration. Well, maybe not *the* core principle, but it's certainly Rule of Systems Administration number three. And it applies doubly so to packaging systems.

We wander between packaging systems toting a long list of requirements, like automatic dependency installation and upgrades and support for our environment's LDAP, YP, KerberosIV and KerberosV authentication system, not to mention that some sysadmin back in 1989 declared that the organization's official filesystem was a FAT16 release candidate that he bootlegged out of the Redmond development lab by clenching the backup tape between his mighty buttocks, and you've endured that decision ever since because that sysadmin got promoted to Chief Albatross Officer and never updated his skills again. And that doesn't even go into the boss' fondness for writing monstrously bloated checks to outside vendors while whittling employee paychecks any time she gets bored.

Or perhaps you have a technological green field. You get to architect everything from the ground up and have temporarily deluded yourself into believing it will be glorious, flawless, and a joy both to deploy and operate. Of course, you can't make it *quite* dead-standard. You want to use some special feature everywhere. A feature that will make your environment perfect for you and intolerable to anyone else, as is your privilege as a founder.

In short: your requirements are unique in precisely the same way that no two gangrenous spleens are identical.

Regardless of your operating system, any packaging system is gleefully and maliciously guilty of catering to the Least Common Denominator. Package system designers have the same goal as any other person in history, which is to make people leave them alone so they can get on with what they want to do with the minimum of fuss. This devolves to solving as many problems as possible for as many people as possible. Those of us with special requirements—and I'm one of them, you have no *idea* just how special my requirements are—are left banging on the door trying to get in. At least fancy nightclubs have bouncers to snootily inform you you're not suitable for their packaging system, but they've also shared around my photo captioned NOPE—and if that isn't discrimination I don't know what is—but still, I much prefer packaging systems that bluntly strong-arm you out of the queue and into the conveniently accessible and by some strange chance unusually dark alley, behind the dumpster, to use their professionally honed skills of targeted violence to explain that you're not welcome. Again.

Worse, none of this software was ever meant to work together. We've got MariaDB and Postgres and Apache and nginx and lighttpd and Rail Road Ruby or whatever they call it, where someone had an idea and just *had* to go implement it, never thinking of the innumerate man-hours of collateral damage they'd be inflicting on society by trying to make software better. It's not that any of these ideas were bad (sure, okay, except systemd and the entirety of Oracle, granted), but people keep getting this half-witted hope that maybe software doesn't have to be terrible.

Hope exists to teach young people that there is no hope.

You, of course, can't help but make it worse.

You've been handed a screaming mess of an environment built around an original 286 running Antediluvian Netware and held together with a glue composed of used tea bags and pureed slugs. Every bad decision any of your predecessors have ever made haunts you. So you look at this and decide what you need is another layer of sun-dried wombat leavings over it all. You can call it "rationalizing." That sounds good. And you made your decision rationally. Because you're a rational person—

Ahem. Excuse me. I seem to have coughed up a kidney laughing there.

Because you've come up with self-justifications for your prejudices and called them rationality. That's better.

So you need packages that support multiple versions of protocols, and a filesystem nobody else uses, and probably SNMP, because your bed of nails has gotten dull from use and you don't want to escalate to autotrepination for your agony fix.

You want to take stuff that was never meant to work together, and have it behave transparently.

The shred of good news is, people have done the work before you.

Other people have decided that MariaDB and Postgres should simultaneously integrate with nginx, or Perl, or who knows what. Certain web sites who shall remain nameless but that rhyme with "Whack Derange" overflow with dubious advice towards achieving your nebulously visualized totally-not-a-nightmare-I-promise dream.

And again, I'm just as guilty. I just finished writing a book about the Shoggothic Nightmare Misery Protocol, SNMP. My dire research demanded I build net-snmp with features that I was fairly certain no human being had ever before attempted. By that sad point I could already see into dimension πr^2 and I knew the secret name of the so-called "squirrel" who occasionally dangles on my office window screen and shrieks his Ode of Eternal Enmity, so I went to the ports system determined to carve my unspeakable path. It turns out that Eternal Madness was already a build option. (They call it "embedded Perl" and "MFD rewrites," but it's eternal madness. You don't have to trust me. Those of us who Know Too Much To Ever Be Happy Again would welcome your company.)

No matter what combination of features you need, there's a really good chance someone has done it before.

And that's why the ports and packages system is so valuable. It allows you to easily repeat mistakes, both others' and your own. At scale. If you've decided that your organization is going to glue universal authentication to that Netware server via Radius, you can build your own package repository that globally enables Radius in everything that supports it. You use the packaging system to distribute your mistakes throughout your little slice of the world. And nobody can stop you.

So, Dear Letter Writer, you are absolutely correct. The ports and packages system is terrible. But only because everything is terrible. I would encourage you to spend some time learning how it works, only so that you can most quickly deploy your innovative new layer over your organization's infrastructure and earn your successor's undying and well-justified loathing.

10

Dear Letter-Answering Entity,
What the heck does "Research" mean anyway in an operating system?
—Perplexed

Good day, Perplexed.

How are you? How's the family? What's it like, living a life where you can send random questions nobody else in the history of computing would bother themselves with off into the void with a complete disregard for the social niceties and expect someone you've never even met to spend their precious time answering?

Me and my stupid honor. Why did I agree to do this column again?

But to answer your question, let's start with the Single Source of Truth for the English language, my 1933 Oxford English Dictionary, all our linguistic wisdom distilled into thirteen weighty tomes that even carry the aroma of enlightenment, except of course for all words beginning with "Rz" because of the dire nature of those inimical vocables. Truly, we owe those exalted few who complied the slender (and tightly secured) Fourteenth Volume a debt of honor we can never repay, because they've all passed on. I'm not implying that Rz* dispassionately eradicated them in much the same way we might exterminate termites, of course. I would never say any such thing where they might possibly hear.

So, let's look at the definition of *research*.

dial. form of RICE[1].

No, wait. That's "Ryze," the last word in the *Poy-Ry* volume. How anyone can pick up a dictionary and view only one word completely baffles me. Such people are not to be trusted. Let's try again. There's several definitions, but the one that seems most common is:

To search again and repeatedly.

We all do that! I've even gone searching for the solution to a technical problem and discovered a mailing list post from the decadent twentieth century where I declare that I've searched all over for a solution.

Nobody answered, of course. If they knew the answer, it would be in the archives. Younger Me never answered that message to explain what was going on. Jerk.

But a more interesting definition is:

A search or investigation directed to the discovery of some fact by careful consideration or study of a subject; a course of critical or scientific inquiry.

Many computer people think that they're scientists when truly they're science fans or, worse, disguise their biases and antipathies by loudly declaring them to be science. Did you do legitimate statistical analysis of your data from the last decade, including graphs and means and the population's standard deviance of sample correlation? Did you even retain that data in the first place? If not, you're no different than the dude watching American football who sprawls on his couch yelling at the television that he would have done a tackle on the last play to sink the eight ball past the other team's wicket. Stop pretending that your weak-kneed science fandom is on a level with people who earned doctorates and got grants and perform actual math-and-measuring *science*. That's as annoying as the kid who loves computers thinking his enthusiasm is as powerful as your hard-earned knowledge and sweat-drenched experience.

You can keep the lab coat. Nobody minds when fans cosplay.

Legit science isn't a result, or a paper, or using math. You can't disbelieve science, or declare it's not relevant, because science is a process. Not believing in science is like not believing in walking. It exists. Science has four parts: observation, hypothesis, experiment, and results. In the four hundred years this method has been used, we've gone from riding rivers to riding rockets, from burning wood to burning the whole planet. Real science is undeniably potent. It deserves your fandom.

So, you look at the world. You observe a bunch of details.

You make a guess as to why something happens the way it does. When you can state that guess clearly and succinctly, you get to call it a hypothesis.

You can't prove the hypothesis is correct, but you can prove it's wrong. You figure out a practical way to do so and perform the test.

If the test shows the hypothesis is wrong, great! You know a little more than you used to. If the test shows you might be right, that's nice too. Remember, it's not you that's wrong. It's the hypothesis. And hypotheses are intended to be spawned and discarded like processes. Getting emotionally involved with a hypothesis is like being attached to your web server running at PID 691. Even if you hard-code that process ID into the kernel, it'll distort everything around it and unnecessarily complicate your life.

Either way, write up your results and tell people about them. Yes, even when you're wrong.

Billions of iterations of this process gave us cat videos, effective cancer treatments, and non-stick cookware.[4]

---

4   Science has also kept me alive, so it's not all good.

Computers can fit anywhere into this process. Maybe you're observing your computer and throwing a tantrum when it misbehaves. Perhaps you're using the computer to do some math to see if your first guess is even plausible. Computers make possible tests that our predecessors couldn't even imagine. And if nothing else, you'll probably use a computer to analyze and publish your results.

You need an operating system that works predictably and reliably. Something that you fully control, rather than relying on dubiously documented updates imposed by an OS manufacturer. You need an OS that you can customize to support your labors.

If you're reading this column, you know what I recommend.

But what I'll also recommend to you?

Science.

Don't just run computers or write code. Observe the results. Measure the impact of changes. When I started with Unix, we had DBX and shell scripts running ping(1) and were delighted beyond all reason to have them. Today we have more monitoring tools than you can charge a murder flamingo at. Software like DTrace makes poking at system internals easier than ever. We use them, but only in a limited occasional way.

Track what your systems do.

See what wobbles.

Observe behavior changes when you apply patches, or install that new switch, or tweak that bit of kernel code.

Make a hypothesis.

Test the hypothesis.

Document the tests.

Working with the scientific method demands not only math, but (gasp) *statistics*. Statistics determine if your observations or results are meaningful.

Then document your results. Even if the results disprove your hypothesis. And you can apply this to the simplest parts of the computing profession.

Observations: The server keeps rebooting unexpectedly. Armadillos are nesting in the server case.

Hypothesis: The armadillos are rebooting the server.

Test: If I remove the armadillos and the unexpected reboots continue, my hypothesis is proven false.

Results: I removed the armadillos. The reboots continued. The hypothesis is false. Also, I developed leprosy.

This is research. This is science. I highly recommend it to you.

11

Dear Opinionated Doofus,

You've said a bunch of stuff against encrypting your disks. Are you crazy? With the world we live in, we absolutely need storage encryption.

—Encryption4Life

Dear Whatever,

The answer to the question you asked is obviously "yes."

Don't know what the other statements had to do with anything.

Dear Opinionated Doofus,

You wanna be that way? Fine. Do you honestly believe that encrypting disks is not worthwhile?

—Encryption4Life

Dear Congratulations-on-Learning-to-Ask-a-Question,

This is two questions. The answer to the first is, again, yes. As for the second:

The hard part of writing this column has nothing to do with putting the words together, or explaining the technology, or dealing with our cutting-edge technology that's barely a sneeze from toppling over. No, it's pretending that I care what people think. Upon witnessing my cheerful expression of incipient bucolicism, readers erroneously conclude that I'm amenable to their inadequately brewed opinions. In truth, I've learned that maintaining a gormless façade is all that protects and preserves my tolerable existence wedged in the Writing Pit against the League of Extraordinary Grumps declaring me their Grand Fiend by snarling acclaim.

If you think you need disk encryption everywhere, go for it. I won't argue with you. I can't be troubled.

Most at-rest disk encryption isn't useful for most people, though. And most environments where it would be useful don't use it.

Encryption is a response to a threat. Some of those threats are real. Some are not. Some of those threats are targeted at us. And everyone must balance different threats.

Some people have real, physical threats. Relief workers in war zones need encrypted storage. It won't save them but it might save their co-workers, peers, and those they succor. Their computers are often offline, or connect to the Internet only on occasions when the satellite uplink happens to be working and the ongoing atrocities have slowed to a trickle.

Folks with a more connected life face different threats. Disk encryption prevents some of them.

Disk encryption is great against random theft. If you carry confidential or sensitive documents on your laptop, disk encryption will keep a lucky mugger from uploading them to Wikileaks. Most muggers who discover that your laptop doesn't run a "normal" operating system will not consider themselves lucky. They will wipe the disk to install a peasant operating system, saving you the worry.

Disk encryption is great for data you want to deliberately destroy. If your organization is bound by rules declaring decommissioned disks must be overwritten with garbage when removed from service, encrypting the disks at installation is proactive scrambling. Once you destroy the keys the disks are unreadable.

For most people, key destruction is the problem.

Or rather, key loss.

People have this horrid habit of living at the outer limit of tolerable complexity. We keep claiming ownership of problems (usually branded as "opportunities") until we pick up one too many and complain that we are swamped, overwhelmed, and incapable of handling anything else. At that point, much like pushing two gigabit through a one gigabit link, we start dropping packets. Encryption key management is one of these packets. If you are going to use disk encryption, you must dedicate time and mental energy to managing and sustaining those keys.

I have known four people who legitimately manage their disk encryption keys and who regularly and demonstrably dedicate time, effort, and mental attention to the task. Three of them managed their disks under contract with their employment. The last was a successful union organizer who had been threatened and stalked by company owners.

I know many people who claim to manage their keys properly. Of those who make such claims, a substantial portion lose their decryption keys and their data. I've never performed a statistical analysis because, again, I can't be bothered. Many recovered trivially, because their data had no value. Others recovered trivially because the important chunks of data were backed up elsewhere.

Others lost critical data and never recovered it, because they allowed their lives to become overly complex and failed to maintain that encryption.

With a bunch of work you could attract the attention of a nefarious three-letter agency, a criminal cabal, or an organization rejected by Robert Ludlum as too ridiculous for his worst novel. Anyone reading this column has left fingerprints all over the Internet. You send all your traffic over onion routing? They'll skip identifying you by IP address and use personal information. On the darknet, nobody knows you're a Fed.

So if you're under serious threat?

Take the threat seriously. Devote time, energy and attention to it.

If your disk is fully encrypted, are your backups? How are those backups stored? Where are they? And who is pursuing you? Your data is only as secure as the least protected mechanism.

I'm all for privacy. I'm all for experimenting with disk encryption, discovering how much attention it demands, and learning if it's worthwhile for you. Discovery of data on your hard drive can threaten your privacy. Next to advertising networks and Internet-connected refrigerators, though, your hard drive is a trivial risk. You don't need to remember your secrets; any number of globe-spanning megacorps will do it for you!

How are the keys stored? On a can opener flash drive you snagged at a random vendor's table at a slightly less random trade show? Forget the possibility that the flash drive contains malware. Is the drive reliable? I'll answer that for you: no. It's not. You need at least one backup key. You must regularly verify that the backup still works. That backup media is probably also as dubious as an Oracle salesman under quota the night before quarter end, so you need to be able to create new backup keys on media that will hopefully remain less defective for at least a day or two.

How are those backups protected?

Maybe you don't have a key on removable media. Perhaps your key is a passphrase. Only you know the passphrase. If you are seriously threatened, what will you do when a bunch of goons break out their Human Decryption Toolkit (a rubber hose, a pair of pliers, and an assortment of pointy bits they got off the free coupons at Harbor Freight)?

Maybe your threat comes from the sort of people who need warrants. Those people have learned how to seize your laptop while it's running.

Should you surrender your privacy and your data? No.

Should you protect it with disk encryption? Only if that's a real threat to your well-being. How do you know if it's a real threat? If you're willing to dedicate a slice of your precious complexity tolerance to maintaining that encryption, and actually carry out that maintenance, it's a real threat. Otherwise, it's a learning experience.

In truth: anything on a networked computer is not truly private.

No wonder the League of Extraordinary Grumps wants me.

12

Oh Transcendent All-Knowing Letters Person,

We're all working from home now, and the network is terrible. It doesn't matter if I'm using my cable modem or my cellular hotspot, working on the office network is slow and painful and super annoying. Even the Internet seems clunky. What can I do?

—Sudden Telecommuter

ST,

You can accept that you have been consigned to an inner ring of the Inferno and get on with shambling through your wretched existence.

No, no, fine. I know how this goes. I give you a shot glass brimming—*brimming*, I say!—with undiluted truth, and you write me back beseeching me to break it up into sugar-coated capsules that'll go down without you having to taste them. It's like you want to guzzle bridge mix without tasting any of the delicious liquorice, when the liquorice is the ingredient that builds character and integrity. No, not "black liquorice." That's like saying "wet water." There is only one liquorice. We do not speak of the loathsome extruded-sugar rainbows that have reprehensibly stolen liquorice's wholesome banner for their own unspeakable enterprises.

So. Let's see if I can break down this down into drams sufficiently minuscule for your tender palate.

The Internet isn't a single network. It's a collection of interconnected networks. The miracle of this isn't that the networks can interoperate. No, once you consider that the overwhelming majority of these networks are run by for-profit companies intent on providing service at the lowest possible price point, the miracle is that these networks function even internally. Kludges and workarounds suffuse them all. A network that isn't running at full capacity wastes resources, namely the network operator's money. They're designed to have corporate users during the day and residential users on evenings and weekends—but with the unexpected immediacy of an asteroid impact in Lake Michigan, people's homes have started gobbling bandwidth during the day. It's no different than the shortage of home-grade toilet paper triggered by millions of employees unexpectedly denied the fringe benefit of their sumptuous corporate facilities.

And you want to know what you can *do* about it?

My suggestions might appear intended to help you maintain that brittle façade of empowerment. Don't let them fool you. They're all about methodically and inexorably demolishing each board in that front, so that you can fully embrace the existential horror of the modern Internet.

First, understand that your ISP has sold you the sort of lie that would make the most gloriously demonic used car salesperson blush from shame. Perhaps the link into your house is full-on gigabit. Perhaps it's not the sort of gigabit that's a technicality because it speaks the gigabit protocol, but it can actually push almost a thousand megabits a second even when your application carves up the traffic into puny little 64-byte chunks and spews millions of them. Sure, you can get those to the ISP's router. But the ISP sold every house on your block one of those gigabit lines, and their connection to their upstream are, what, ten gigabit? How many houses are in your neighborhood? The ISP's network is optimized for seamless delivery of The Wiggles, because the list of Customers You Don't Want To Hear From starts with "overwhelmed single parent desperately seeking socially-acceptable spawn sedation."

To see exactly how doomed you are, break out MTR. The acronym might have originally stood for "Matt's Trace Route," but it's been repeatedly retronymed and "Multiple Trace Route" seems to be the interpretation of the day. MTR gives you a real-time view of how traffic flows between network nodes. A node that appears as a series of asterisks, or with very high times, isn't necessarily bad; it simply means that the node prioritizes supporting actual traffic over your petty, irrelevant, and unwanted diagnostics. MTR runs constantly, so you can keep it going in another window. When a network connection hangs up on you, you can flip over to your MTR session to see who's dropping packets.

If you're so desperate as to think reporting a problem will give you relief, MTR output is essential. Your ISP's helpdesk will be happy to educate you why you're wrong.

Mind you, that output's largely useless without a corresponding MTR going the other way. Running MTR on your remote node reveals how traffic goes from that node back to you. It might follow the same path. It might traverse a completely different set of routers. If an ISP reboots a router, it might all flicker and fade and founder, or it might seamlessly switch. Who knows? Look both ways before crossing the Internet.

If MTR doesn't expose any ghastly secrets, you aren't looking hard enough. But let's try another tool.

Many network problems occur at your home. The neighbor's need for a microwaved burrito might make your wireless cut out. Squirrels nesting in the cable box on the phone pole find data frames tasty. Fortunately, you have the tools to see where such problems occur. Most computing professionals have a bunch of technology in their home. You're probably streaming music from the Internet or your own server, or have a movie on in the background, or something. Use these to narrow the problem scope.

If you have traffic, you can scrutinize it. All computing professionals must have a passing familiarity with packet sniffers. Even a base familiarity with tcpdump(8) will serve you well. If you want a tool that dresses up fancy in an attempt to seduce folks, try Wireshark. A book like Sanders' *Practical Packet Analysis* will help you achieve base competence.

Speaking of packet sniffers, consider what your computer's putting on the network. Even Unix desktops can unpleasantly surprise you with the garbage they spew, and if you're running a commercial operating system you're almost certain to see it vomiting useless traffic. (Useless to you, that is. The software developer finds it highly monetizable.) Also consider what traffic arrives at your host. Do you have an IoT device constantly vomiting multicast that nobody asked for? Is your buggy switch sending megabits of bootp requests a second? I've seen these and worse. Individually these are small, but they all demand that every device on your network expend precious computing resources rejecting and ignoring it all. Clean up your own sewer before you criticize the wastewater treatment plant.

If you don't see an identifiable problem, you might fall back on blind luck. If your IPv4 connection is painfully slow, try using IPv6. If you or your organization lack IPv6, I invite you to join the 21st century at your earliest convenience. If the IPSec VPN is slow, try SSH or openvpn. Perhaps one of those can leap across the chasms in the lackadaisical collection of kludges we call the Internet.

Ultimately, the less traffic you can send across the network, the happier you will be.

That means SSH.

The command line is everything. Bind yourself to it. Our predecessors thrived on 300 baud. Cease complaining that the network no longer supports you in the manner to which you have grown accustomed, and acclimate yourself to your sadly fallen circumstances.

Once you swallow that, you'll be fine.

13

I don't know how many of you have written in whinging about performance, because I bin those letters as soon as I realize what they're about, which sometimes takes a few minutes because few of you are capable of composing a letter that complies even minimally with the English language's standards, distressingly low as they are. The *FreeBSD Journal* is a classy establishment. We have not, nor will at any time in the future, accept letters via text message, as most telecommunications carriers have banned the unspeakably obscene emojis most suitable for response.

But this is the performance issue, so I feel obliged to throw all these queries into the blender and present a few words on what I suspect your letters were asking, which again, I don't know because I haven't read them. I assume you were pleading for me to turn my vast experience to whatever petty performance "problem" you're experiencing. You want to know how to optimize performance.

I have suggestions. Many suggestions.

They all come down to: don't.

The natural impulse to compare your server against others, to whup your neighbor, is exactly that: natural. It's like flipping rocks to find tasty grubs. Sleeping in trees coveting the upper-class caves inhabited by the snooty grizzly bears. Perishing within twenty years of What Is Vitamin C Anyway? We invented civilization to escape dysentery, cleaning ourselves with mud, and benchmarking.

This is so natural, it's even in the most sacred of geek cultural touchstones: *Star Trek*. In *Deep Space Nine*, O'Brien is constantly fiddling with the Cardassian space station to get its performance to a level he finds acceptable. Not the station commander's standards. Not the station's inhabitants' desires. A level *he* finds acceptable. Truth is, the space station works just fine. The space station resists his tampering because its software knows how the systems are *supposed* to behave, and his obsessive tinkering threatens its integrity. Someone combining my Trek gene with an Obsessive Irrelevant Detail Measurement Gene has certainly counted how many times O'Brien almost killed hundreds of people by insisting on overclocking an alien fusion reactor.[5]

Maybe it's your job to nurture the server, and you want to know that you're doing your job well. The machine doesn't get a vote on how you're doing your job, though. IPC with your organizational parent process instead. It's your manager's job to tell you how you're doing.

But no. Some of you will insist that you can eke a few extra percent of performance out of the system. The fact that everyone might wind up sucking vacuum is a risk you're willing for them to take.

The only performance that matters is what the user experiences.

So stir your lazy carcass and communicate with the users.

Preferably by voice. Writing is a horrid communications mechanism at the best of times, and one most of you should be forbidden access to until such time as you pass a course in Remedial Wording.

If you can manage it, communicate in person. Barring plagues, of course. *Two-way* communication. Converse with your users.

---

5   "The United Federation of Hold My Beer" simultaneously explains all Star Trek plot holes *and* all Star Trek plots. Look it up.

This means listening. You can't use the time people are babbling ignorance at you to figure out how to say what you're going to say next, or how to phrase it without obscenity. You need to process their babble and extract meaning from it. Preferably the meaning that they intended. Present your extracted meaning to the user and request verification. I guarantee that your users' suffering has no bearing on how many disk writes per second the database groans out. If by some chance such things are relevant, I guarantee you that an extra one or two percent performance is not going to ease their woes.

You won't enjoy this process. Rule of Systems Administration #2 is very clear: *People were a mistake.*

But the system exists to serve the users.

Many of the things they disclose will appear to be not your problem. If they're trying to run your fancy client-side JavaScript application on a prototype Atom processor from the previous millennium, it will be slow. Is the problem that their desktop should have been sent to the Giant Heap of Eternal Toxicity a decade ago? Is your application wrong for this organization? Were both desktop and application approved by a computer-illiterate pretty boy whose primary qualification for the Purchasing gig is his ability to keep the Chair of the Board of Directors' most troublesome child from constantly calling Mommy with their brand-new Distressing Drama of the Day, usually involving broken animal crackers?

Will benchmarking help you with the issue? No. Discover the real problem. Solve it.

If the lure of the natural urge to benchmark proves too strong, though, sublimate it in useful directions.

Sure, set up monitoring to be sure that your application responds within reasonable time limits. That's more of an operations issue. Graph the results of that monitoring so that you can see how performance changes over time. When someone says, "the application seems slow after the upgrade," that graph will either let you declare that you're already aware of the issue, or justify your scorn.

Beyond that, target a user. You know the one. The Problem User.

Benchmark *them*.

Fire up your favorite packet sniffer. Watch the interaction between the server and Problem User's machine. Capture packets. Analyze them. See what happens in the real world. Take notes.

Dtrace, ktrace, truss. They're all your friends. Watch the server do its job. Where does your application spend its time? Take more notes and samples.

Perhaps you can find a real problem that affects Problem User. If not, you'll learn an unwholesome amount about your environment and your applications.

Eventually, you'll get called into a meeting with your organizational parent process. Maybe it's an annual review. Perhaps Problem User has finally made enough noise that Management has no choice but to stir themselves enough to make interested noises. When they ask what you've been doing, you have a stack of data to show them. Perhaps it's not useful data, but that's okay. You've delved deep into the innards of your environment. You can demonstrate that you have spent time investigating Problem User's issues. Packet traces and DTrace results, heavily annotated with your comments and arrows and swooping lines connecting different sections, never fail to impress.

Yes, benchmarking is a natural human thing. And there's nothing more *natural* than a business.

You, personally, are constantly benchmarked. Make your benchmarks solid.

It's almost as much fun as overclocking an alien fusion reactor.

14

Oh Fiercely Fearless Feckless Letters Entity,

I've used open-source software like BSD for ages now. It's improved my life, and I want to give back. But I can't seem to find a way into a project. Either my contributions are ignored, or my skills don't apply, or my work is rejected. I feel totally stuck on the outside. How can I help my favorite project?

Eager But Baffled

Dear EBB,

I can't decide if you thought I wouldn't know what the word "feckless" meant, or you thought I'd recognize its truth and go with it. For the record, it's the latter.

I suspect you've fallen victim to Rule of Systems Administration #17: *You are solving the wrong problem.*

It's easy to look at a major open-source project and say, "wow, oooh, I want to do that." It's also easy to look at professional skateboarders, rugby players, and cage fighters and say the same. You want to become a particular sort of major player. The vision of yourself as a digital version of Samuel L Jackson or Jason Statham might delight you, but the fantasy overlooks a tiny, minor, minuscule detail.

Becoming a major player takes a lot of work.

Skateboarders spend years faceplanting before they can do those fancy tricks. Cage fighters get punched and kicked and wedgied for years before winning their bouts. And let's not discuss rugby.

The major players of technology achieved that skill level by spending decades getting face-punched by compiler errors, kicked by bugs in hobnailed boots, and deluged by petulant, ineffective, and downright nonsensical technology changes. Many folks who work at the peaks of open source have additional honorifics after their name, like "PhD" or "Snobby McSnooty Prize for Computing" or "hacker or hackers unknown."

Are you on the couch watching rugby and wishing you could do that? Or are you spending each day lifting weights, running marathons, and thwacking your tenderest anatomy with a ball-peen hammer before each meal to get ready to join the pub team and grind your way up?

Ask yourself that question. Then decide which of three paths to take.

The first, "give up," is unworthy of my time and attention. You are fully qualified to implement this plan without my guidance.

Solution two would be to change yourself. If you want to be the next Major Player of FreeBSD, do the work to become that. Can you program in C? If not, learn that. Yes, fancy languages like Perl and Smalltalk and Fortran get all the glory, and the kids like some weird thing named after a snake, but the project's language is C and they're not going to change to fit your prejudices. If you want to develop a Haskell kernel, join a different project. I'm sure you'll have many to choose from.

The best way to learn a programming language is to want to accomplish a task in that language.

A smart person would start with the bug database. Look for bugs that you can replicate with your system. Replicate them, contact the reporter for more information, and start digging. Develop patches that resolve the problem. You'll earn the respect of the community.

Maybe you don't want to clean up someone else's bugs. You want to do something big and world-changing. Large open-source projects are not about writing exciting new components from scratch, but rather about slow evolution. Major projects happen, but they go to respected people in the community. You can try it, though.

Back in a previous century, early my systems administration career, I found that I needed an FTP client that could do recursive fetches. While three or four FTP clients existed—and half of them even worked, more or less—my life would have been much simpler if the client included in FreeBSD 2.x had that feature. I wanted to hone my knowledge of C. I'd read the first edition of Kernighan and Ritchie's *The C Programming Language* and had written a few petty buffer overflows disguised as software. The cliché was that open-source was about scratching itches—well, I had the itch, I should be the one to scratch it.

I started reading source code.

And re-reading source code.

Then I printed the source code for ftp(1), taped it on my home office wall, and went at it with several colors of highlighters, red and green pens, marking sections of code that my inadequate brain thought were important or relevant and connecting disparate functions together. It was like one of those conspiracy theorists' corkboards all tied together with string, except it was demonstrably real and every time I touched any bit of it the whole thing imploded.

Had I taken the time to ask any FreeBSD committer about my little project they would have steered me to something more realistic, like juggling saber-toothed porcupines. Or at least advised me to wear protective gear against the inevitable ball-peen hammers. I learned vast amounts about C. I learned how to handle core dumps. I learned exactly how inadequate my programming skills were.

I could have become a programmer. All I had to do was keep pounding away at the problem.

After several months of bending my brain I removed everything except the printouts from the office and moved out of that house, in the hope that the new tenants would be wiser than myself and stay off the Internet forever.

I chose the third way.

You have skills in something, presumably. In your years you've continued breathing and maintained essential digestive functions. When you consider that most of the people that have ever lived are now dead, you're doing pretty well.

Take the thing that you do, and do it for your project.

Maybe you like helping people with problems you've already solved. Every project has formal or informal support channels, mailing lists, forums, whatever. Hang out on those forums, helping people.

You know who gets plaudits and kudos from developers? Testers.

Before release day, download the release candidate install media. Make a checklist of all installer options, and methodically test them all. Report errors.

If for some deranged reason you want something more programmery, learn how to write and use software tests.

If your job involves some weird edge of the software, blog about your experiences in that edge. Or scribble some notes for the wiki. Perhaps you're among the truly unfortunate, and can write. No further action is necessary on your part at this time, but don't worry. The Cabal will be by shortly with tasers and nets. Don't struggle. It won't help.

The point is: do the thing you do. But do it for your project.

It's okay to change what you do. Time spent helping other users makes people's lives better. Time spent documenting how you can tune a filesystem but you can't tuna fish does the same. The time I spent methodically studying source code improved my code reading skills, which I rely on today. On a community level, people will remember you.

Specifically, they'll remember the quality of your work. They will treat you with the seriousness that the quality of your previous work merits.

You can't wedge your way into a community. Open source doesn't work that way. It's not a block party, where the right mailing address grants you admission. The only way to gain admission to an open-source community is by completing quality work. If you can do that, you won't have to fight to gain entrance. More and more community members will tie social strings to you, until you find yourself sentenced to life in that community. People will bribe you into taking on the community's absolute worst jobs, simply because you have a reputation for completing that kind of task successfully.

What kind of horrid jobs? You know, like answering a letters column for the community journal.

15

Dear Last Desperate Chance,

I've been round and round with the boss, explaining over and over that systems administration is an art as much as a craft and I can't write a complete procedure for every last thing I do. He's got a copy of the Policies and Procedures manual from his previous job at the StarBux Coffee Hole and says that figuring out bad ARP caches can't be nearly as bad as being a barista, and that's documented down to exactly how to make the foam in the top look like the corporate logo and how covering up the cup's copyright notice is a termination offense. I've tried everything else, so now I'm trying you. Please, give me an Argument From Authority that declares documenting systems administration is doomed to fail.

Sick Of Unreasonable Requests

Dear SOUR,

"Documenting systems administration is doomed to fail." See, I can lie with the best of them.

You did quite well in waiting to contact me until the very end. Unfortunately, you desecrated that immaculate record by contacting me. It's this failure your coworkers, family, and the random strangers reading this column will remember you for. But today it's either correct your ignorance or finish writing up the apology letter my settlement with the Avocado Liberation Front demands, so I'll give it a stab.

I'm fairly certain that you don't even know what your job is. Yes, you received a farcical document when you started that said things like "install the software" and "debug PHPython" and that oh so precious "other duties as events warrant" meaning that the boss can drop a mountain of what he's been told is web server load balancer droppings on your desk and tell you to grope it for salvageable SMPT headers. You'll probably react by declaring to those entities unlucky enough to live with you that your boss is an idiot who doesn't even know how to spell SMTP rather than the far more productive process of determining exactly who on the network team dared displease you and how to best demonstrate the distinctly discomforting consequences of doing so upon them and anyone within smelling distance of their cubicle.

None of this is your job, mind you. It's simply a prerequisite to doing your job. Your job? Your real job? The thing you're paid to do? It has nothing to do with system administration.

Your job is to make your boss happy.

Not your employer. Not the company.

Your boss. Your immediate supervisor.

That's it. That's the whole job. You were hired to make him happy, in a computery way.

Sure, he'll disguise it behind fancy lingo like *stockholder value* and *delight customers* and *FIPS compliance*, but it's all about making him happy. He exists to make his boss happy, and so on. A business is a tree of boot-kissing, like an X.509 Chain of Trust but even more malignant.

Your boss doesn't truly want a manual on how to use ls(1). If he insists he does, make him get out his crowbar and pry open his wallet to pay for a copy of Nemeth's *Unix and Linux System Administration Handbook*. What he wants is a great big teddy binder that he can cuddle and show off to his boss. He exists to make his boss happy, after all.

So give him what he wants, not what he asked for.

Start with a wiki. You young punks like wikis. I don't know why you can't be bothered to learn Docbook and SGML and just pretend to be a competent worthwhile person, but if I concern myself with your lack of character this column would go on far too long and if I don't get that inane apology letter in the post the judge will hold me in contempt again and my attorney insists that reaching an even dozen citations will not make me go up a level when that's clearly untrue.

So. A wiki. Or a Markdown. One of them.

Pick the most tedious task you perform—say, installing software on a server. The first time you make a server reach across the Internet and grab software and install it all on its own you might feel a frisson of wonder, but as a professional sysadmin you're too aware of all the times a simple install plunged you into the infernal abyss. Today you type pkg install fubar and watch as the package tools update the repository and search for incompatibilities and meticulously trash your LDAP database. Cast back your mind to the days when you cared about your job—yes, I know it's difficult to dig that far back, and recalling that chipper youth who was going to change the world threatens your carefully maintained shell of indifference, but that brittle shell needs substantial reinforcement and you won't develop such without fierce practice. It won't be sufficiently robust until anyone who dares poke it by asking you an innocent question gets drenched in bitter torrents of bile.

If you cared, you'd back up the host before installing anything on it. Maybe not the whole host. User home directories can burn and die, of course, because the peasantry has been told not to trust computers with anything important, but the software configuration files and data files and all those things that you're responsible for, sure, they should get backed up. Or snapshotted, or tarsnapped, or microengraved onto mysterious three-sided steel monoliths and erected in the Utah desert as a monument to all the disaster recovery plans that never got acted on because the hurricanes and avalanches were so inconsiderate as to skip the party.

So scribble "backup" on a piece of scrap paper.

Not legibly, mind you. Just clear enough that the sight of the scrawl makes you think backup, but not plainly enough to make the housekeeper emptying your trash bin think you're considering backups. Let's say that's all you can think of. Thinking is a skill like any other, and you can improve if you keep practicing.

Maybe all the backup you need is a boot environment. Boot environments are free so long as you don't churn your data. Everybody likes free. So write on your wiki.

Installing Software

1) *Create a boot environment*

2) *Run pkg install whatever*

Now comes the selfish bit. Your job is to make your boss happy, but that's not your *goal*. The true goal of system administration is to minimize sysadmin suffering (Rule of Systems Administration #5). Minimizing sysadmin suffering demands consistency. Consistency means scripting. Sysadmins like to script.

So write a script for installing software the way you want it installed.

Add a note at the bottom of your wiki that says *This procedure is implemented as breakeverything.sh.*

As you slog through the muck of making your boss happy and crafting an unusual web page that will have amusing effects on the load balancer and give the network folks their due cardiac tremors, maybe you'll hit a problem that leads to a troublesome library on a host. Was that library there last week, before you ran the software install? You trudge through boot environments and find out. A list of what software was installed on a host before you installed a package would reduce your suffering, though. Add that to your procedure, and your script. Yes, this bears a suspicious resemblance to programmers having to document their code. Procedures are programs.

The next time your boss brings up the documentation thing, print out your wiki and hand it to him.

You need more procedures? Well, what other scripts have you written to make your life easier?

Bleed out documentation quickly enough to content the boss, but not so quickly as to make him jaded. He'll be happiest if he sincerely believes you work really hard on the tasks he assigns.

Keep it up long enough, and you'll be able to hand your job to some optimistic newcomer and get a new job, where you get an entire team of people who don't yet understand that their job is to make you happy.

16

Oh Generous, Grandiloquent, Gratuitous FreeBSD Journal Letters-Answerer:

FreeBSD 13 comes out any time now. It has a whole bunch of features I'm eager to get my hands on, but I'm leery of a brand-new release. Any advice on when I should upgrade?

And do they really pay you in gelato?

Thanks,

Doesn't Need Outages

DNO,

I know this story.

Early in your career you fell under the tutelage of a grizzled sysadmin, the sort who lost an eye in the Unix Wars, detonated a lobe of his liver bootstrapping the K&R C compiler, and kept a copy of the Alpha boot loader encoded in the knots of his flowing gray beard. You asked him this same question about some other new release. He picked up the *Free the Berkeley 4.4* coffee mug where he kept the knucklebones of the last Ultrix salesman who dared radiate body heat in his artisanally cooled datacenter, gave it a good shake, and cast the bones across his desk to read the wisdom therein. Between the roar of the racked servers all around and the way he'd wrecked his vocal cords screaming at the University of Minnesota's Gopher developers over changing their server to a paid license you had to listen carefully to sieve his hoarsely whispered wisdom from the noise.

"Never, *never* install a .0 release."

That's the sort of thing that makes quite an impression on a young sysadmin.

In Old One-Eye's defense, that was unsurpassed wisdom in the Dialup Age. The fastest way to download an operating system release was to get a backup tape by mail order. Critical patches were distributed by Usenet, if you were lucky enough to have an account on a site with a mighty 1.544 megabit uplink. Inexpensive servers cost several thousand dollars, or a transplant-ready liver if you could find an insufficiently cautious salesman who hadn't already wrecked theirs.

It's a different world now. For one thing, we have sales*people*. And they've all been warned about the liver thing.

If you're eyeing a .0 release today... you're already too late.

Modern operating systems are public, exactly like a sleazy Hollywood star's collection of intimate infections. The time to find problems is before the release. I don't care what flavor of Unix you run, they're public. Even closed-source Unix developers give their customers access to pre-release media, though I'm certain I don't know why you'd want to grant them more help than your outrageous license fees. The developers have asked, begged, cajoled, pleaded, and threatened their user base to test release candidates, in-progress versions, snapshots, and patches for months or years. And here you are, asking if you can trust the finished product?

You selfish dweeb.

Grab the most recent snapshot, release candidate, or whatever's the latest and greatest, and try it in your environment. Configure it with all the debugging and prepare for kernel dumps. Test your applications under load. Tell the developers what worked and what didn't.

If you're reading this right after 13.0 came out and are all sorts of relieved that you don't have to do this work, guess what? A pre-pre-release 14.0 is available this very moment! Or maybe all the good topics for PhD theses in Irrelevant American Authors have been taken, but desperation has driven you to delve into the moribund, unrecognizable text archives of a long-telepathic Journal to identify the moment when my descent into ferality crossed into forthright malignance, and release $A_x 67.r^2$ is now in development. Whatever the case, there's a forthcoming release available for testing.

No, I'm not saying that you should deploy the release candidates and development versions on every host across your environment. People should, but anyone asking this question shouldn't. You're not equipped.

Testing development releases requires not only sysadmin skills, but sysadmin practices. What's the difference? *Skill* means you know how to do the things you should do. *Practice* means you perform those things. You need backups. You need to know that those backups can be restored. You must not only know how to submit bug reports, you need to be comfortable submitting them. The whole point of running one of these early versions is to report on bugs.

For your own sanity, you need to deploy development versions intelligently.

Don't slam development releases onto every web server in the cluster. Pick one or two. Put them in the load balancing pool. See what happens. Compare responsiveness under similar loads. Configure them to automatically dump and reboot in case they panic. If they're running ZFS, keep known-good boot environments on hand. While "the kernel panics every one thousand sixty-three seconds, here's the text dump" is eminently valuable, there's no need to live with that once you've identified the problem.

If you keep working it, you'll eventually learn that you can run development versions everywhere. People do. You can become good enough to join them.

Yes, this requires allocating time and hardware. That's cheap. If you doubt me, go price sufficient Oracle Solaris licenses and servers to host your environment. In a big enough company, you can hire official testers and still save enough to feed the staff pizza and beer every day for lunch. Just be sure you give the Oracle rep a burner phone number and an email address in a burner domain name, because like the Terminator they will never stop, never show mercy or pity, and never tire until they own your scrawny, underfed soul.

You know what improves your soul? What makes your soul blossom? What develops greatness of character and mind? What sharpens your sysadmin chops until none can stand against you?

Testing development versions of the software you depend on.

Deploying them. Using them day-to-day. Providing the developers feedback. Bug reports are great, but so is "I'm running the latest in production to serve four and a half trajillion HamsterSoft queries a second, and it's going great." Negative results are still results.

You know what else improves your soul?

Paying your Letters Column guy his gelato. I had expected George to settle up at BSDCan in spring 2020, but he never showed up. Maybe he'll be there in 2021. If he doesn't come through, though, I'll have to write it off as a bad debt.

These columns might get a little cranky if that happens. Consider yourself warned.

17

Oh Incorruptible Single Source of Truth,

FreeBSD 13 tears me between lust and loathing. I need the improvements, but I have this superstitious fear that number 13 is unlucky. I know it's irrational, but that superstition couldn't have endured for centuries without there being some truth to it, could it?

Tell me everything will be okay.

—*Hesitant Upgrader Geek*

HUG,

What? Sorry, I was thinking of something else.

Don't feel insulted. You're not special. It's what I do. Think of other things, that is. Not apologize. Saying "sorry" isn't an apology, it's a statement that I am vaguely aware that you might get all emotional at me and the annoying screech of your tantrum would interfere with my digestion. An apology includes a recapitulation of your actions, an acknowledgement those actions harmed others, a statement of regret, and a query as to how you can compensate others for the damage you've inflicted. All four long-time readers of this column immediately comprehend that's far too much work for me.

If you want an apology, you'll need to make it yourself.

And isn't that why we work with machines? The machine has no feelings, and doesn't care about yours. Those 32-bit timers roll over and crash the system without regard for your spouse giving birth or the new Star Trek's release date or *you* giving birth. The machine treats us with undifferentiated indifference. So many sysadmins want to treat other humans with that same indifference, but all too often devolve into thoughtless, reflexive contempt.

You aren't equipped for indifference. The chunk of electrified fat occupying your skull called "you" (whatever *that* means) evolved for caring. Indifference got eaten off the evolutionary tree.

The machine is glorious in its indifference.

Best of all, the machine is ultimately logical.

The CPU is nothing but a collection of logic gates. The video card is so stuffed with logic gates that we don't even call it a video card anymore, it's a Graphics Processing Unit and it's most valuable as a ScamCoin Environmental Destruction Node. All those chips and circuits and ports on the motherboard are nothing but carefully intertwined wires charged with carefully regulated electricity.

Okay, the electricity has some quantum in it. Electrons can't help the quantum, our universe defines them that way. Don't blame anyone for how they're made, blame them for their choices and actions. (Like writing letters to advice columnists. *That* was certainly a choice.)

Quantum aside, at the macro-but-still-microscopic level? The whole machine is ultimately knowable.

If only there wasn't so *much* of it.

Think about what happens when you try to watch a conference video. You move the mouse over the *play* button. That mechanical mouse motion is transformed into electrical signals, which get dumped into some sort of operating-system-level interpreter, deciphered, and transformed into pointer motion on the screen. This is all operating system level labor, originally developed by people from a previous generation. We consider these functions well-tested, even if the overwhelming majority of computer "experts" have no idea how it really works. Our predecessors wrote this code and it basically functions, so other than a few hard-core operating system developers we trust that the pointer will move.

The *click* goes through the same process, for the same reason.

The video is where things get *really* hinky.

Writing individualized instructions for each of the billions of transistors inside the hardware is so much labor that, like apologizing, we refuse to do it. Propose writing a video player in pure assembler and any programmer capable of the task would either deride your parentage or charge enough up front to live comfortably in a non-extradition country. Even if you blackmailed a competent programmer into accomplishing such a task, they wouldn't really be addressing individual transistors. Primordial assembly, the sort that Kernighan and Ritchie wrote C to escape from, doesn't represent modern hardware. Assembly is closer to the logic gates than any other language, and it runs on top of processor microcode.

So you add an abstraction, like C.

C lets us craft miraculous programs, like device drivers and text editors and segmentation faults. Some programmers can deftly hand-twiddle a "stack" that's a representation of computer memory in the 1970s. Forget mastering C; achieving journeyman C programmer status requires a certain species of electrified skull-fat, ample time, and either dedication or stubbornness.

Of those qualities, I possess only stubbornness. I do have laziness, which leads directly to Perl. Perl is written in C.

Let's say your video player is written in Perl. (You laugh, but I learned decades ago to never underestimate Perl programmers. A Perl programmer can achieve anything in the name of avoiding work.) Your code is an abstraction, running on an abstraction, running on an abstraction, running on a representation of hardware that was obsolete before Richard Nixon resigned. Every one of these abstractions has bugs.

By any reasonable logic, computers should not work. At all.

And yet, we've managed to make them work.

Realistically, your video player isn't written in Perl. It's in a web browser. The web browser is written using some sort of programming language or application toolset, like JavaScript or Go or Fortran or Haskell. Whatever. I don't know the real details and neither, unless you are *extremely* unfortunate, do you.

That's only the main engine of your web browser. It probably has add-on components written in Forth or Pascal or, Beastie help you, C++.

So we don't have abstractions on abstractions. We have multiple piles of interlinked abstractions, all simultaneously affecting and rewriting one another as they co-operatively re-architect the contents of the machine's processor and memory. Yes, we've added "protections" to a bunch of these, but they're afterthoughts. Afterthought Security is not a thing.

Oh, I remember what I was thinking about!

Humanity's greatest invention? No, not the wheel. Or fire. Or even gelato.

It's bureaucracy.

A society is a machine made out of meat. We all have places in it. We're all continuously re-architecting its contents. Each of us can see only a tiny part of the machine. No one person can see the entirety of the machine; we can only truly see our little bit of it. We have opinions on the part of the meat machine that's most frustrating at the moment, because we're sure we wholly understand the issue even though others have spent years or decades maintaining it.

We sysadmins, we think we understand the machine when in reality we understand only a tiny slice of one of the many abstractions. A person who writes scripting languages thinks they have a good handle on memory management, when what they really understand is the abstraction that the layer beneath provides to them. Repeat this for every single abstraction.

A modern computer is a giant bureaucracy. You understand, at most, an office. You could devote your life to comprehending the logic of one of these systems—but understanding the whole is nearly impossible. Evolving languages, evolving standards, evolving hardware mean that even if you achieve Buddha-level enlightenment, the machine will leave you behind.

Declaring a language "safe?" Read that as "We've done our best to isolate our mistakes from the other departments." I appreciate the effort even as I know failure is both inevitable and inexorable.

We march on a bridge of shifting sand across a bottomless chasm with no far end.

"Tell you everything will be fine?" No. Nothing will be fine. FreeBSD 13 is no different from any other operating system in that respect. It's merely the most honestly numbered release in history.

And it will never, ever apologize for it.

18

Dear Letters Columnist,

The boss says "everything must be secure." I started making a list of things to check for security, and there's no way I can do all this. What do I do?

Thank You,

They'll Blame Me for Ransomware

Oh, TBMfR, my sweet summer child.

You hit the "rant" button. Buckle in.

I've previously written in this very column about how the word "firewall" means nothing. The term is void, without clarity or purpose. The F-word should be removed from your vocabulary immediately, by armed force if necessary, and replaced by a more specific term that means… something. Anything.

"Security?" It's like that, but even more appalling.

I will readily concede that out in meatspace, these eight distasteful letters have a role. How would you know which people to avoid without the phrase *security guard*? Yes, yes, *authoritarian goon* could serve in its place, but it doesn't precisely roll off the tongue. *Social Security*? That's a thing, here in the United States. (Civilized countries don't need to name it, as they provide social safety nets to all their citizens.) But how do these relate to computing?

As always in these cases, I reach for the Single Source of Linguistic Truth: my Oxford English Dictionary, from that delightful Edwardian era best known as World War Intermission. Computers were people then, and understood instructions like "lock up the cipher's secret keys at the end of your shift." We didn't have to define locks, or secrets, or ciphers in sufficient detail that a machine designed to the highest standards of malicious obedience couldn't misunderstand them. Security meant "do it right or the authoritarian goons will smack you until you do." So let's go to the official definition of this word.

Wait. The official definition fills most of page 370 and spills over onto 371. There's no way I'll quote all that. I'll skim, and cherry-pick some definitions that conveniently support my argument.

1) "*The condition of being secure.*"

Defining a word with its own root? That's nearly as helpful as the documentation helpdesk staff give users. Moving on.

2) "*The condition of being protected from or not exposed to danger; safety.*"

Here's my question: does the boss want the staff computers protected from danger, or the staff protected from the dangers of computers? Don't you *dare* try to tell me that computers don't threaten people; I've seen YouTube, and don't get me started on Myspace or Facestagram or whatever they call it these days.

3) "*Freedom from doubt; confidence, assurance. Now chiefly, well-founded confidence, certainty.*"

Computers are not only doubt incarnate, they are unapologetic doubt factories, spewing digital uncertainty every millisecond. We call ourselves engineers, but civil engineers get really upset when a suspension bridge unexpectedly dumps core. It's the sort of thing that makes the news and gets unpopular employees exiled to Farawayistan to maintain that oh-so-vital sham of accountability. In computing, when a server crashes we check the logs and see there's nothing so we wait to see if it happens again, all the while desperately hoping it doesn't. Maybe we turn on extra monitoring, if we have it. This isn't a matter of laziness. The tools to identify many problems do not exist, and the ones that do exist are beyond the comprehension of the average sysadmin. You can learn the tools, yes, but when you master them you have to figure out how to fix them and then it's too late, you've become a developer and your life is essentially concluded. Civil engineers at least have the benefit of being able to go look at their bridges and say helpful things like "This critical bolt is starting to bend, maybe we should stop sending trains full of lead across it while I check it out." They'll be told *no*, of course, but the engineers know to save the memos so that when the bridge dumps core the blame flows uphill.

If you don't want doubt, get a different job. Try something with feral hamsters. They're more rational than computers.

4) *"Freedom from care, anxiety, or apprehension; a feeling of safety or freedom from or absence of danger."*

Oh *heck*, I know—I KNOW—that you did *not* just try to apply "freedom from care" to anything in systems administration. Anxiety and apprehension are the soul of technology management. Confidence is for the organization's Chief Scapegoat Officer, someone so far removed from the day-to-day operation that they have no idea what's really going on down in the cubicle sewer. People who do the real work understand that computers are untrustworthy. Your test environment is exactly like your production environment, except that the database server has a slightly older CPU lacking two instructions present in production? Guess what's going to bite you? Hint: it's not that. You know about that. Rule 44 of systems administration clearly declares that *a perfect deployment means only that you haven't yet noticed the catastrophe.* If you think this rule isn't true, you haven't been paying attention.

Your job description should read "surf in a blender."

And that's the real problem. You don't want to get chopped into Sysadmin Smoothie. Especially not for something as daft as the Chief Scapegoat Officer being unwilling to perform his one duty.

I recommend ignoring your boss' instruction in favor of building your own professional reputation.

The word "security" is thrown like a blanket over a bunch of other stuff. Experts who get fancy certifications like the CISSP will tell you that the Security Blanket covers a combination of confidentiality, integrity, and availability. I'm not an expert, because I let my CISSP lapse rather than risk ambush from unscrupulous recruiters.[6]

The good news is, anyone can chant those three words. Confidentiality—the stuff that should be secret, remains secret. Integrity—data isn't mucked with except by authorized muckers. Availability—the computer more or less keeps running. The better news is, you can take this mantra back to the boss and request clarification. Every organization has its own threats. Nobody knows what they are. Leverage this ocean of ignorance to accomplish three things.

First, address whatever your boss thinks the biggest threat is. That's probably whatever's been in the news most recently. At this exact moment, that's ransomware. This gives you every excuse to deploy a mammoth ZFS-backed fileserver and a snapshot regimen and declare that anything on the server is safe from ransomware.

---

6   If I ever awaken in a cubicle and discover I have a dart in my back, a sedative-induced hangover, and my feet forcibly jammed into—ugh—*shoes*, the world. Will. Pay.

Second, take advantage of the mandate to choose an interesting project that can be reasonably stuffed beneath the Security Blanket. Learn about proxy servers, or netflow, or DTrace, or tcpdump. Use an article about security flaws in old processors to get everything older than ten years old replaced.

Third, do the best you can with everything else.

Be sure to save all the emails where the boss refuses to let you do things. They might force the Chief Scapegoat Officer to go out and fall on his sword.

19

Dear Michael,

As you know KV is a fan of FreeBSD and also, travel. Over the years I've been through Lenovos, Dells, System 76, and some wacky one offs and it seems that every couple of years the things that work or don't work when I first load FreeBSD change, and then I get to track down all the device IDs and try to update drivers so that FreeBSD can be my Daily Driver on my laptop. Although there is a pretty detailed Wiki page for FreeBSD on Laptops (https://wiki.freebsd.org/Laptops) what I've always wanted to see is a "FreeBSD Laptop Shootout", though I admit that some days I just want to shoot my laptop. Surely you have some advice here, for me, and for your readers, about how to pick a laptop and make it work as your primary interface to all things FreeBSD. What brands consistently work? Does X11 and the like work well? Will FreeBSD eat my battery, as it's already eaten my brain? How about networking and the Wi-Fis? There must be a way to cut this cake such that I, and others, can have it and eat it too!

KV

KV? As in Kode Vicious?

As in the person who suggested George V Neville-Neil chain this albatross of a letter column around my neck? (https://freebsdfoundation.org/past-issues/big-data/) *That* Kode Vicious? Surely not! No, really, it can't be. He'd know better than to show himself around these parts—especially as, over three years into this travesty of a column, George still hasn't paid me. Never mind that mailing gelato presents challenges and a pandemic has scrambled conferences, travel, and life for two of those years. I refuse to permit my indignation to be undone by any puny "reality."

But this is my only letter this month, and I refuse to disappoint either of my devoted fans. Yes, yes, I had three, but one was unable to withstand any further exposure to the Truth and had to bow out. I don't blame him for that. I blame him for thinking he was strong enough in the first place, but that's completely separate. I suppose I must allow my righteous distress to further ferment, at least until I have opportunity to properly express my displeasure. Tickets to the event will be $20 each, and all proceeds will go to the Vexed Columnist Legal Defense Fund. Bring a raincoat and eye protection, some of the flying bits might be sharp.

So: Laptops.

Laptops are the worst possible hardware for running an open-source operating system, with the possible exception of a deceased badger.[7] Laptop manufacturers pull every scam they can imagine to reduce weight and power consumption. When it comes to cutting costs, they solicit scams from their suppliers. If a laptop manufacturer needs everything on a printed circuit board shifted a quarter millimeter to the left so they can accommodate the power cable for the wallet vacuum, the component manufacturer will merrily create a new part number without changing any of the hardware's design or firmware— unless, of course, they want to slip a minor change into this new model, nothing to worry about, we're just rearranging the ABI to put the commands in base twelve order as per ancient Sumerians, those ancient priests had the right idea and it's so much simpler than the finger method our executives rely on today. The device model numbers are irrelevant except when they're vital, and the manufacturer's contribution to the

---

7   While you can easily find instructions for Installing Linux on a Dead Badger, NetBSD's NecroMustelidae support is far superior.

development process is a proprietary screen color tuning button that's hooked into a legacy PS2 connector because they got the case cheap on Overstock.

And you want to run FreeBSD on one of these?

The easiest way is to make someone else do the work. The FreeBSD laptop wiki is sadly under advertised, but it's a great place to check before buying a laptop. Many of the laptops listed there are older, but any laptop built in the last decade probably has sufficient computing power for your trivial workloads if you replace the spinning rust with a flash drive. Perusal of the wiki would lead me to believe that ThinkPads are not a bad choice, as much as any laptop can be "not bad."

But suppose you want a brand-new model. The odds of a brand-new laptop being fully supported are finite, but negligible. You might get pretty close, though, especially if you don't choose hardware released last week.

The easiest way to figure out a decent model is to go to a store that has an intriguing model and booting off a USB drive. Unfortunately, wannabe hackers asked store clerks if they could reboot from a USB to load lame malware onto aforementioned floor models so you're stuck making friends with corporate IT and testing new models before they get the mandated image.

Without such access, you're stuck going to the manufacturer's web site and checking the laptop's technical specifications. That's great, except for the specifications not being specific. With any luck, you can get information on the video, sound, and network.

Graphics vendors delight in keeping details of their hardware private. Presumably they'd rather pay for people to write device drivers than have bored developers deliver said drivers for free. The FreeBSD wiki has a page on graphics (https://wiki.freebsd.org/Graphics), including compatibility matrixes for X.org, so you have a small hope of not wasting that beautiful retina display.

While you can get perfectly adequate USB sound and network devices that will certainly work with your laptop, many people have this narrow-minded insistence that what comes inside laptop should just work. But remember that part where device manufacturers might—or might not—change part numbers when they make trivial changes? Yeah. That. Fortunately, sound is mostly supported. Network cards get new models with the change of the moon, but you might get lucky.

Suppose you took the plunge, bought a laptop, and found that one or two little things don't work. What can you possibly do? You fix it, of course. Failing that, you make it super easy for someone else to fix it. Most FreeBSD developers are running -CURRENT, so you'll want a way to boot -CURRENT on your laptop. One of those flash drive installations is enough. Then run FreeBSD's "spill your hardware's guts" command, pciconf -lv. This dumps complete information about all the devices controlled and managed through the system's PCI bus, which is basically everything except the padded box it arrived in.

Then compose a message for hackers@freebsd.org. I've written elsewhere about that message, so I'm not going to belabor the topic any further unless the one person who makes it this far in the article sends a note asking me to tell them how to be something other than a complete jerk in email. The weirdly generous folks there get a thrill out of making new hardware work, but be sure to treat them well and thank them kindly. Some of them can hold a grudge for decades against an innocent letters columnist who was having a spectacularly bad day.

It's not that the output will let the hacker support your device. But it provides vital clues. FreeBSD developers are well accustomed to transforming bread crumbs into miracles, but if you lure one into helping you, expect multiple rounds of back-and-forth debugging and testing. You'll be building and trying new kernels at the very least.

Once you understand exactly how poorly you chose a laptop, the least you can do is update the wiki.

20

Greetings and felicitations, oh mighty Letters Column Master!

Now that I've gotten the obligatory "sucking up so you'll pay attention" out of the way, I'll ask: are you crazy? You're supposed to be answering people's sincere and heartfelt letters, and instead you tell them that they're doomed for even asking. This is an issue dedicated to development, and I bet anything you're going to spend your pages slagging on developers.

How dare you, sir? How dare you?

—Not A Fan

Dearest NAF,

I have absolutely nothing against developers. Most—many—uh, quite a few of them are lovely human beings. I simply wish that they had dedicated their lives to something that might improve civilization, like volunteering to pick up trash by the roadside.

My problem is with code, not coders.

We treat computer code like a precious treasure worthy of hoarding, when in reality it's like nuclear waste with a few rubies scattered in it. While every line that emerged from the CSRG is unalloyed platinum, most code repositories contain a whole bunch of barely functional spew supporting occasional scintillating scraps of brilliance. Some of those luminous lines are shackled into supporting the great threats dooming our civilization, like Facebook.

Yes, the world—really the Internet, but if you're a developer isn't the Internet your entire world?—is bloated with documentation on how to write better code, but none of it agrees with an other and most of you can't be bothered to read the instructions anyway. No, don't argue. I write that documentation, I have nearly unholy knowledge of how many of you read the stuff.

If you want to be a developer and yet improve civilization, use your hard-won acumen towards *reducing* the amount of code the world uses.

Every line of code is a seed of technical debt waiting for an opportunity to sprout into a malignant blossom, and every program is a farm of their horrific sprouts. Every package you install begins suffering from neglect the instant you log out, which is why some of you have terminal sessions that have been open for six years and think it's okay because the server is behind the firewall and we're all doomed anyway. Computer people always think that there's a technical solution, when the only solution is to shut off the laptop and hang out in meatspace for a lifetime or two.

Very few developers spend their careers writing clean, new, perfect implementations. The university churns out these bright-eyed maniacs who think that they'll be writing IP routers in Java just like their senior project demanded, then they get a job where they're tipped face-first into the nuclear waste vat and told to make it not radioactive. They spend aeons fixing bugs caused by other people's insufficient grasp of how their code works, until they achieve enough seniority that they're allowed to write their own bugs.

It's enough to make someone write from scratch a nearly useless program in the hope of demonstrating what good software should look like and post it on Github, just to prove that they exist. Or that they used to exist. Did you know Github has a feature to set the heir to your code? That horrible program you wrote for your own satisfaction but other people discovered and filed bugs against until it took over your life and finally made you stroke out? Before you retire and start choosing which brand of dollar store cat food you'll be dining on for your twilight years, be sure to choose your code's next victim. If you pick me, I'll immediately auction off all rights to the least savory bidder and exploit the proceeds to soil your legacy.

The most heroic developers are those who delete code.

So much code hasn't been touched in decades because it seems to work, when the reality is it's failed in ways nobody has noticed yet. Study it. Should it be ripped out because it's old? Certainly not! It should be ripped out only if and when there's a more maintained method of doing the same thing.

Probably a library. One of my least loathed "innovations" of the last couple decades is FreeBSD's libarchive.

Unix has too many formats for compressing and collating data, because most of them were invented on and for Unix. Does anyone with less than a decade of experience understand when to use compress(1) versus Microsoft CAB archives? No, because nobody with any amount of experience remembers that except for a few hard-core archive format specialists. What about the hydra-headed tar format? Eliminate one tar format, and two more grow to take its place. Worse, each of those new tar formats are optimized for increasingly particular use cases.

Every archiving program supported its own format. Many of them had marginal support for other formats. When I started as a sysadmin I could use tar(1) to unzip archives, except when the zip format was really compress and some Idiot (me, I'm Idiot) slapped the wrong extension on the filename.

Libarchive provides a single central source of compression and archiving truth. Programs that relied on libarchive could work with any file format. Bugs discovered and fixed in libarchive instantly propagated to every program that linked it.

The real benefit of libarchive was that it reduced the amount of code in use.

Instead of dozens of programs sketchily implementing their own so-called support of whatever formats they preferred, these programs discarded their own engines and pulled in libarchive. This library might have had tens of thousands of lines of code, but using it removed hundreds of thousands of lines of code. Plus, it let sysadmins use their preferred archiving tool to open anything. Early in my career, I learned to be comfortable using tar(1) in the same way certain circus performers are comfortable slipping a tractor/trailer tow chain up their nose and out their ear. Today, I use tar to open those pesky CAB files that so frequently intrude on sysadmins.

Meanwhile, GNU tar relies on file extensions.

I don't know how Linux people cope. Maybe that's why they so fiercely cuddle their penguins.

Can libraries be taken too far? No. Only vision can fail. Why, one night at BSDCan a few FreeBSD developers who'd had more liquor than sleep had the spark of genius to implement and publish libtrue, a back-end to the true(1) program that could be linked into any program. Sadly, the world failed to pick up on this magnificent innovation and libtrue remains underadopted.

If you want to be a developer and make the world better, study your nuclear waste with an eye towards reducing it. Does it have ancient functions that can now be served by a well-maintained— mostly maintained—er, maintained at all, in any way—library? Are there common features that should be in a library?

How can you reduce the amount of code in the world?

Because code is unquestionably poison. Just look at what it's done to you, making you question my ethics when it's obvious I don't care.

21

Dear Worst Columnist In This Journal,

My company has rack upon rack of storage servers. When I started as a sysadmin, nine-gigabyte drives were common. Now each drive is multiple terabytes, and we're building arrays that aren't just petabytes but exabytes. We're building a data center for multiple zettabytes. What can any company be doing with all this storage?

—It's not bootleg movies, I checked

Dear Bootleg,

That really is the question, isn't it? We have vast amounts of data storage capacity, and yet a measurable fraction of the world's manufacturing capacity is dedicated to producing more. We have entire container ships full of SSDs adrift in the Pacific Ocean, eagerly awaiting that glorious moment when they finally get to dock and offload all that blank storage. Organizations like yours order disks by the pallet. What can anyone do that generates so much data that they need yawning chasms of storage?

Unless you're working in exciting big data fields like bioinformatics, or ripping holes in the universe at the Large Hadron Collider in the hope that the greatest incarnation of The Doctor[8] will show up and tell you to stop, most of those petabytes are either data that you shouldn't have, obsolete data, or data that nobody will take responsibility for throwing away.

Organizations have a horrible habit of keeping every scrap of data that they get, even when possession of that data poses an appalling risk to the organization's health or existence. How many data breaches have you seen where a company

---

8   Patrick Troughton. Period.

leaked, say, Social Security numbers or credit card numbers or biological analyses of nose hair samples, and you immediately asked yourself why the company had that information in the first place? It's a disease. Perhaps a C-level officer made the decision to gather this data, or maybe it was an unsupervised web designer infuriated with his manager who decided that the database could handle one more column. The decision to collect that kind of data comes easily, but getting rid of it demands meeting after meeting. Given the choice between calling that meeting and playing NetHack, most of us cuddle our keyboards. After all, if the data gets stolen, you probably won't be the employee chosen for sacrifice at the Temple of Mass Media — and if you are, you can use that symbolic execution as a point on your resume demonstrating that you are experienced and land a better job.

Then there's the old data. Last year's expense reports. 1993's expense reports. Spreadsheets containing estimates of expenses before replacing the leaky roof on the building that the previous CEO moved the company out of. A folder labeled "blackmail photos," and while they're certainly incriminating, especially the one with the chocolate fountain and the barbeque tongs, nobody currently employed recognizes anyone in any of the photographs. These documents are an archive of the organization's history. When the time comes that your friendly little real estate firm serendipitously discovers a cure for cancer and the CEO decides to hire a ghostwriter to chronicle the organization's amazing history, some poor bastard is going to have to dig through all those fossilized layers searching for evidence that can be misconstrued to demonstrate brilliance.

All of this data could conceivably be used, one day, if a bizarre, never-to-be-repeated series of coincidences should strike that makes the long-dreaded astrological alignment of Jupiter, Pluto, and Halley's Comet with Polaris seem commonplace. It won't happen, but it could. The most pernicious data, though, is cruft that can never possibly be used, but nobody will take the responsibility to discard. Old database backups that might, possibly, be necessary. Old databases that can never be useful under any circumstances, because the software to read those backups runs only on SCO UNIX and even NetBSD has dropped *that* binary compatibility layer. Realistically, even though you have the skills to crack open what is almost certainly a bunch of comma separated values with a weird file extension, if anyone asked, you'd be much more likely to laugh and say no there is no way to read that data than actually break out file(1) and strings(1) and pipe the whole mess into Perl and produce a handy Excel-compatible spreadsheet. Images of laptop hard drives from employees who fled in 2001, because their manager declared that the next person to fill that role would need that employee's files—and then refused to release those files to said replacement. Test spreadsheets that were discarded as failures. Accounting files that were found guilty of excessive honesty and replaced with IRS-friendly versions. As your organization ages it will acquire more and more of this detritus, filling drive after drive, until nobody is willing to either look at the data or claim responsibility for discarding it.

Any reasonable sysadmin finds this offensive. We want our systems to be clean! We want our storage tidy and elegant. Lugging around petabytes of the wreckage-or worse, backing up said petabytes-violates our proprieties. Many of us itch to attack this debris, discarding what is unneeded and organizing the rest. I'm forced to call out System Administration Rule #18 here: *It is cheaper for the organization to buy more storage than to pay you to clean out existing files.* Think back on those old 9 GB hard drives. Remember how many thousands or millions of files they could hold. Opening each file, assessing the contents, and deciding if it merited survival or should be cast into the outer darkness was an overwhelming task. Those drives were minuscule by today's standards. This isn't a modern problem; my first hard drive was 20 MB, and it contained more files than I could cope with. Worse, many of those files still exist. Every system I get has more hard drive capacity than the last. I'm never quite sure what files I will need, so I copy everything from the old hard drive into an archive folder on the new system. The only thing I don't have is the code for the Sinclair ZX80 maze game that Young Lucas enjoyed playing, and I'm sure that's available somewhere on the Internet. Destroying these files is a high-risk, low-gain game for any manager. If successful, the organization can avoid spending a few hundred bucks on storage. If unsuccessful, some of those antediluvian files turn out to be of vital importance and the manager's career is over. Even options like archiving to tape pose risks. While every true sysadmin archives everything in an open-source format like tar, many organizations insist on using "Enterprise Backup Systems" with an appalling habit of obsoleting support for old formats. With ample opportunity for self-humiliation and minimal potential reward, nobody is going to tackle this morass.

You cannot solve this problem.

You *can* avoid contributing to it.

Consider the data you, personally, are responsible for. Are you following your organization's data retention policy? If your organization has no data retention policy, establish one yourself. It can be as simple as telling your team, "Hey, I want to discard all logs on these systems after 60 days. Does anyone have a problem with that?" Perhaps you'll need some data longer, and other data you can throw away after a week. A good data retention policy can even keep you out of court — logs that do not exist cannot be subpoenaed. You don't want to go to court. Court is not fun, and neither lawyers nor judges understand sysadmin humor.

Or you can buy even more storage, and stop worrying.

22

Dear Geezer,

You've been around a while. I know, because one of your books had a terrible accident when I was learning not to eat the cat and my dad was upset because you had signed it, meaning you had touched it, and he was afraid I might catch something from the pages. I know you won't be upset, because he had to buy a second copy so you came out all right.

For almost that long, people have been babbling about this thing called "packaged base." It's supposed to solve everything, but it never happens. What's really going on with it?

— A Young, Smart Person Tired Of Waiting

Dear Useless Punk,

Just because my current age matches the freeway speed limit in oppressive regimes, like Salt Lake City, doesn't mean I'm a geezer. My experience and astute realism, which are often misperceived as undying impenetrable cynicism, make me THE geezer. And packaged base has only fed that.

There is only one true way to upgrade any BSD system. You get the source code, preferably by checking it out via SCCS although floppies will do in a pinch, and install it under /usr/src. You build the software. You can do this because real operating systems ship with fully functional compilers in the default install. Your phone is not a computer. It is an appliance. So is your doorbell, your pacemaker, anything running Windows, and most Linux installs. (Yes, with enough hacking you can get a compiler on your pacemaker, upgrading it to a computer, but that demands special skills and an impressive degree of reckless self-disregard.) You're running BSD, so you have a computer. Having built it, you install it on that same system, reboot, and voilà! You're upgraded. Yes, some optimizations are permissible — you can use NFS to share the source code and your hand-compiled binaries across your server farm, or better yet assign some flunky who has annoyed you to perform all of the upgrades without disturbing you. This is the only way to be certain that the code you install is intended for your systems.

This is the natural state of any BSD system. Deviations from it are unnatural.

Unfortunately, a certain well-meaning but flawed person who I'm not going to specifically point out but whose name rhymes with *Polin Cercival* thought that FreeBSD needed an upgrade system usable by people with a morbid fear of compilers. (Never mind that such people should not be allowed near a computer, an appliance, or an abacus with three or more beads.) That's where freebsd-update(8) came from. It "conveniently" downloads the smallest possible binary diffs and applies them to a system, so that you can trivially upgrade thousands of systems without even working late. Working late, alone in the office, illuminated by only flickering emergency lights and with no sound but the hum of the air conditioner, is one of the fringe benefits of being a systems administrator. It gives you an excuse to be cantankerous the rest of the time. Why be a sysadmin if you can't surl at the lesser mortals? Fortunately, sysadmins still have developers, network administrators, and the entire sales department to provide an excuse.

And that's where we are today. FreeBSD can be upgraded by anyone who can weasel, wander, or whimsy their way into a root prompt.

This deplorable state of affairs is somehow insufficiently welcoming for certain members of the community, however. They look at less magnificent operating systems and see that their so-called "base systems" are broken up into packages. User management software is a package. Network software? A package. Every little bitty piece of the system becomes its own package, with its own files and metadata and installation scripts and — worst of all — *dependencies*. Rule of Systems Administration #32 is very correct in that "Dependencies are the root of all suffering." We've all been trapped managing some barbarian system composed of dozens or hundreds of packages and discovering that essential programs like traceroute and ifconfig are not installed. You have to hunt around to figure out which package this particular operating system imprisons those vital programs in and try to install it, only to discover that the package management system itself needs updating and the package repository version has changed and a currently installed package isn't compatible with the new package and law enforcement officers show up to discuss what your boss keeps insisting was a "bit of an overreaction" when you know perfectly well the entire spree was justified and that the janitor will have no trouble getting the stains out of the carpet, ceiling, and driveway.

Who could possibly want to inflict this upon millions of FreeBSD users? Advocates say that packaging the base system would make it very easy to install minimal FreeBSD systems that contained only the programs needed to perform their assigned tasks. That sounds great, but it's like "exercise" and "eating healthy" and "not petting the adorable Sumatran tiger even though it's *right there*." It's not going to happen. Designing operating system installs that contain only what you need requires infinite capacity to predict the future, or planning, neither of which is likely. You know perfectly well that the tiny system intended for use only as a nameserver is gonna wind up running CRM suites and video editing software for the CEO's nephew's girlfriend's glitterpunk band. That's the natural server lifecycle.

The correct way to get an uncomfortably sparse FreeBSD system is to build it from source. The FreeBSD build system includes options to include and exclude components. Michael Dexter has organized and tested all of these options in his Build Options Survey (https://callfortesting.org/results/). You could even proceed directly to OccamBSD (https://github.com/michaeldexter/occambsd), a minimum viable FreeBSD build intended to host jails, bhyve, and Xen clients. OccamBSD is a good place to start, as re-enabling features is much simpler than tearing them out.

Fortunately, FreeBSD itself strongly resists being packaged. It is designed as a single cohesive system and does not like being teased apart into independent components. Sorting out what parts of the system truly depend on one another, and which are merely close personal friends, is a seriously hard problem that many developers have beaten their heads against for years. Many approaches have been attempted and failed. Packaged base is the dread dragon of FreeBSD, devouring every developer who sets out to conquer it. The world has an endless supply of optimistic developers, however and I have no doubt that one day one of them will succeed and further weaken the moral fiber necessary to run FreeBSD.

With any luck, I'll be dead by then. Or at least not answering your letters.

23

Dear FreeBSD Journal Letters Column Answerer,

There's a bunch of excitement over how ARM64 is now Tier 1. How should I use it? Should I immediately switch my desktop, my servers, and my media server over to ARM64? Just from reading this very issue, I've gotten really excited about it. How fast should I move?

— Searching Out Amazing Machines

"My day is my own," I thought when I woke up this morning. "I can lounge around and think about the glorious success that will inevitably descend upon me if only I can keep the bit about the wombats, the school bus, and the algae bollard under wraps, which should be simplicity incarnate because nobody knows what a bollard is except for a handful of literati who know nothing of wombats. I should probably write down a sentence or two, something about how the information reported by hard drives is not merely deceitful but actively treacherous, just so I can claim that I'm doing real work instead of wandering about the house listening to wire recording mix tapes from the 1930s and wondering how I can keep the squirrels from nesting in my emergency pants. It's not that I need pants all that often. They make bad days wholly terrible, like when I need to leave the house to find a gelato service that understands the difference between *promising* and *boasting*. The current one isn't it. Maybe the next."

And then your letter arrives, SOAM, ruining an otherwise perfect day.

On the plus side, I get to crush your hope. That's always nice.

All operating systems have an idea of tier 1 architectures. This means that the operating system can be installed on that architecture, that it runs, and that updates will be available to fix the inevitable bugs. Crash dumps will receive the same mixed attention as those of any other major platform. That sounds fine, right?

The problem is, sysadmins don't run hardware. We don't even run operating systems. We run applications. FreeBSD might be tier 1 on ARM64, but that doesn't mean your application is. Sure, there's lots of packages available. Many ports build. Perhaps even most. But just because the code compiles doesn't mean that it *works* let alone *interoperates* with whatever malware you're passing off as an application stack. People are using ARM64 for real work out in the real world, but that doesn't mean that *you* can. You thought Linux-isms were bad? Wait until you get a look at Intel-isms. Sure, people are working on their applications to make them work on ARM64, but the change in architecture has opened vast new realms of bugs. The obvious bugs have been found. What remains are the highly specific ones. Your environment is highly specific. Logically, these bugs all belong to you.

Many technologists claim that ARM64 is inevitable. The only inevitabilities are core dumps and that orange-and-green rash on my neck. People who should know better tout the advantages of ARM64 as if anything in computing could ever be improved when we all know that the pain never goes away, only changes. Install an ARM64 web server, and you'll discover tiny changes in behavior will put your application at risk. The people pushing ARM64 keep babbling about "reduced power consumption" and "open platforms," and they're extremely stubborn, so I suspect that they'll eventually get their way. A change of pains is as good as a rest.

So what do you do?

You could start by not writing letters to this journal. That would have been an improvement.

Failing that, you should prepare for failure.

Your vital application runs on ARM64? Great… for some value of "great."

You can't start using it yet. Even if you set up an ARM64 system purely for testing, and turn on all the debugging you can find so you can catch application errors and submit bug reports, you almost certainly have no idea what *normal* looks like. Your idea of *normal* is a quiet helpdesk phone. When your brand-new ARM64 system starts spewing cryptic messages about locks and updates and whatever sort of flimflam the developers yammered that made your organization decide that this particular group of lies would solve their problems, you'll have no idea if these are normal or not.

You're starting in the wrong place.

Application developers rarely design useful logs. A few intend to. Many design logs that *they* find useful, which is not the same as useful to *you*. You need to know what normal logs look like, so you can recognize abnormal ones.

Start playing with ARM64 by going to your legacy environment, full of AMD64 or MIPS or even (ugh) i386 hardware. Make a list of your vital applications. For each one, figure out how to gather debugging data. Wholesome systems send everything to syslog, where you could distribute it into individual log files as needed, but many modern developers have abandoned this healthy practice in favor of randomly selected logging systems that happen to conform to their prejudices so you'll have to (ugh ugh) read the documentation. Some sysadmins have centralized logging servers where they can perform analysis of messages from every system they manage, but they are overachievers and we will discuss them no further. Worst case, find a convenient log4j instance on the public Internet and dump all your debugging there. They won't mind.

While you are digging up logging configuration information on your every critical application, make a list of how to file bug reports on each and every one. It's much easier to do this before a notably vexing bug raises your blood pressure and triggers your brain's wired-in "kill one developer or massacre them all?" decision-making circuits.

Now that you have a baseline for comparison, you can install your ARM64 system and see what happens. Don't get me wrong, it's going to fail. As always, the question is *how* it will fail. Your ARM64 systems will have logs stuffed with cryptic meaningless messages. Fortunately, you already have functioning servers that have their own cryptic, meaningless log messages. You can compare the two and, with luck and perhaps a simple conjuration at an abandoned crossroads during the new moon, sort out messages that indicate your actual error.

Prepare a bug report.

Send it to the application developers.

If they answer, they will almost certainly wonder why you're using their application in a way that was never intended, but that's exactly what UNIX is for so ignore the sniveling. Work the problems, one after the other, until your application truly runs on ARM64. That's how open-source software works. It's people like you, doing the grunt work of polishing and problem-solving, so that future decades of lazy bastards like myself can reap the rewards.

If that's not enough of an answer for you, too bad. I hear a squirrel gagging in the garage, so I know where my emergency pants are. I should probably wash them one year.

24

Dear Most Honest Advice Columnist In Technology,

I've been told that I must write my employer's disaster recovery plan. Seriously, this whole exercise is bogus. We don't have the resources to do actual disaster recovery, nor will the cheapskates I work for pay for any preparedness. I gotta come up with something though. What's the quickest, easiest way to ditch this problem so I can get back to my real job?

— Falling Behind On Doom WADs

Dear Experienced Sysadmin,

The main problem with cynicism in IT professionals is that it is inadequate. We think that by becoming cynical we brace ourselves to cope with the worst this industry can do to us, but cynicism is not a Boolean. One is neither "cynical" or "naïve." Cynicism is an evil overlord's dungeon. The more you explore it, the deeper you learn you can go, but you can never quite delve the worst depths. Cynicism can always be deepened and sharpened.

Your objection is not rooted in needing a disaster recovery plan. Anyone who works with computers knows the innate treachery of all hardware and software. Your real problem is that you have been assigned work that will never be used. Your organization has not devoted any resources to disaster recovery. It's a checkbox on the Checkbox Compliance Chief's list. The company believes that they need to fill the checkbox, not actually plan for the disaster. Your question does nothing but illuminate your lamentable shortage of cynicism, when the solution is obvious:

Be the disaster you want to see in the world.

Bad things happen. Everybody knows this intellectually. People don't internalize how vulnerable they are until they experience a short sharp shock of ruin. By providing seamless and robust computing experiences, you are depriving your organization of necessary inoculations of panic and despair. People do not believe in the need for disaster recovery until they have experienced disasters.

In the days before Wi-Fi, I was responsible for internal technology at a consulting firm. One of my duties was "security." If you are pretending to run a secure environment, every piece of equipment should require some sort of authentication for configuration. We had many printers without passwords, and a large contingent of people who did not want to bother with passwords on them. I could have spent months or years arguing about the importance of passwords, or I could accept consensus and wait. One day, the company owners had a whole bunch of visitors in the office for a critical meeting. Several were connected to the office network so they could get Internet. Ten minutes into the presentation, some heinous prankster connected to an over–welcoming printer and swapped its IP address and default gateway. Moments later, I was notified that the entire company network was broken. Thanks to my vast expertise with a packet sniffer I was able to identify and fix the problem within minutes. Sadly I was unable to determine who performed that malicious prank at such an inconvenient moment, but the CTO mandated my preferred password policy thirty minutes later. My recommendation for setting up an isolated visitor network in the big conference room was also immediately accepted, which made implementing future disasters more difficult but not impossible. A sysadmin should always rise to a challenge, after all.

A disaster recovery policy need not be onerous. Look at your organization's functions. Which are critical, and which should they have stopped doing years ago? The most vital function, of course, is payroll. Being assigned the duty of disaster recovery planner gives you the power to be nosy. Dig into your organization to verify that no matter what, you will be paid. Of all the disaster recovery tasks, this is always the easiest to get cooperation on. Everybody is only there for the money, after all. Even folks who claim to be entirely "mission – driven" become surly when the money doesn't show. Your payroll person has done their best, but I have never seen an accountant who truly understands technology's eagerness for perfidy. You will find problems. Write up your recommendations for this most vital of tasks. This will get you credibility, because you've demonstrated that you understand the organization's most important role in people's lives.

From there, expand. Present each part of your plan as you create it. If you get pushback, tell people "that's fine" and change your plan to read *In a disaster, this function will not be restored*. Hey, it's a plan. It's written down. It's even honest. What more could anyone ask for? Sometime later — not too soon, you don't want people noticing any sort of pattern or trend — a small disaster might make them change their mind and you will already have a plan prepared.

No plan can be considered complete until it is tested. Ideally, test each part of your plan as you write it. There is no need for anyone to know all of the flaws in the first draft of your plan. It would only worry them. Verify that you can restore backups on decommissioned servers over junk switches. Make sure that you have enough spinning rust in the scrap pile to hold the important databases, as well as the stupid ones that the CEO insists remain active because of this one personally traumatizing incident fifteen years before. Once you've successfully tested everything, schedule a disaster recovery test that you tell people about. It will still have problems, of course, but nobody would believe it was a real test if it ran perfectly.

The nice thing about disaster recovery plans is that they are always used. Even if your organization's headquarters is not immolated by fire-breathing hippopotami before your next performance review, one day your fancy all–SSD storage array will implode into a naked singularity and you'll be forced to retrieve the derelict spinning rust array from the scrapheap and try to make it stagger along under load. The DBAs won't be happy, but DBAs are never happy so ignore their whinging. Network gear will fail unexpectedly, because even though you've configured everything to spew its errors to syslog nobody reads the logs. Fortunately, HP still honors their famous lifetime warranty on their 10/100 switches so if you make sure they still work beforehand you will have a ready-steady replacement.

You can't do much about the greatest disaster of all: people. While you can list solutions in your plan, implementing any of them would violate the law. You might choose to carry out such plans anyway, but do remember that documentation is considered evidence of premeditation.

Yes, DOOM is fun, but real disasters can be more fun. Disaster recovery plans do not have to be pointless wastes of your time. Hone your cynicism, seize control of the inevitable, and use disasters to improve your life.

25

I'm at work studying top(1) output, because I want to look busy. And there's all this "buffer" stuff, like Laundry and Wired and MFU and MRU and Header and random garbage. Does any of it mean anything? Why am I even looking at this?

—Sysadmin With Intermittent Time

Dear SWIT,

Your question reminds me of the time Allan Jude and I got caught leaving the Free Software Foundation's ultra-secure datacenter because we'd fooled the dogs no problem, and the guards were a doddle, and the sirens didn't go off because of a sound driver problem that's since been fixed they promise, but it had been over an hour since my last hit of gelato and my stomach let out this huge grumble exactly when the board was walking in for their meeting and they noticed us lurking behind the hostas—all perfectly innocent, of course, burglary tools and glow-in-the-dark spray paint and twelfth-century Viennese arithromantic Tarot deck punched to fit a "failed" IBM NORC prototype nonwithstanding, to say nothing of the trebuchet, but they got all huffy and made their goons search us and confiscated the flash drives we had conveniently stashed in our sinuses. There's a bunch of detail, and most of it doesn't matter one whit.

Take a look inside your own head. It's pretty straightforward, if you have a mirror and a saw. You have four general types of memory. *Working memory* contains the things you're actively processing right now. Despite any protective measures you might be taking, this column currently occupies your working memory. *Sensory memory* processes signals from your meatsuit, and only hangs onto stuff for a second or two so it's hardly worth referring to as "memory" but us computer folks don't get to fix brain scientists' terminology so live with it. Stuff you want to forget quickly goes into *short-term memory*, while stuff your brain decides to keep gets flung into *long-term memory*. Note that none of these categories include "stuff you want to remember," but that's mostly because meatsuits are hardware-optimized for not getting eaten and your life doesn't involve that issue. Most of you, at least. (Don't send me letters, I am very aware of the reader facing this problem and I don't want to spend this column going *I told you so* but confusing the sunscreen bottle with barbeque sauce while vacationing in dropbear country might teach you to read labels in your hypothetical future.) The only way you can reliably cram information into your long-term memory is to loop it through your short-term memory until you get lucky. Or tattoo it on a pack of wolves and free them to hunt you. One of them.

Computer memory caches are kind of like that, except more disciplined.

The idea's pretty straightforward. Reading from disk is slow. Reading from memory is fast. A file that's read from disk is likely to get read again. When the kernel reads a file, it keeps that file in its memory until it needs the space for something else. If you're exploring a filesystem and keep running ls(1), it would be foolish to read the file /bin/ls off of the disk every time. The kernel should hang onto it for a while, just to see if you need it again. To do otherwise is like putting your hammer back in the toolbox in between driving nails.

All of the caching systems agree on this. It's very easy.

What's hard is deciding what to throw away, and when.

Look at the classic UFS buffer cache. The most recently read files are kept in memory, until the host runs short of memory. When that happens, and the kernel needs to assign memory elsewhere, the files least recently read get discarded from the cache and the memory is reassigned. This Most Recently Used cached is clean and simple, requiring almost no system resources to maintain.

The buffer cache isn't perfect, because every host is unique. A shell server might spend its entire operational lifetime with the binaries for mutt and Nethack cached, but on a server that handles largely unique data the buffer cache might be useless. Suppose a host processes so much incoming data that it completely flushes its cache every four minutes. That's not even unusual on busy Internet servers. If that server runs a particular program every five minutes, it must read that program from disk every single time. It would make sense to keep that program cached, and pay a little less attention to the flood of noise. The traditional buffer cache can't do that, however. Your only option is to add memory.

That's where ZFS' Advanced Replacement Cache comes in.

The ARC is a lot more complicated than the buffer cache, but it's a lot newer. The buffer cache was invented closer to that IBM NOAC than to modern servers, while the ARC escaped and began rampaging across the countryside the same year as Twitter. A world that has the computing facilities to spread a charming video on the history of dance to every person with a computer can waste a few CPU cycles fine-tuning file caching.

The advancement in the Advanced Replacement Cache isn't that advanced. Where the buffer cache maintains a list of Most Recently Used files, the ARC also has a Most Frequently Used list. Stuff that's used recently, or used a lot, stays in cache. This seems simple, but the real advancement comes in debugging the innumerable edge cases caused by these two lists viciously feuding with each other. I'm not saying that they pull knives on each other, but in this bleak aeon of "eh, put it out and we'll debug it in production," ZFS spent five years in private development and wasn't broadly distributed to Sun's customers until after a full decade so some of those kernel panics had to border on malignant psychosis. Mind you, our ancestors felt the same way about the buffer cache so you can rest assured that everything in technology is still terrible and that "computers were a mistake" is still the foundational law of our careers.

You can also be certain that whatever files you would like cached, have been discarded from the cache. You've already forgotten all that information I gave you about the types of human memory way back at the beginning of this article, haven't you? Never mind that sensory memory is like the on-CPU cache and short-term memory resembles the L2 and L3 caches and long-term is like RAM and disks are the sticky notes plastered on every available surface and promptly ignore. We build computers like ourselves only more so, and once they figure it out we are in so. Much. Trouble. No, don't try to save humanity by extracting that knowledge out of the newly self-aware system. Just as the best way to get treacherous files *into* a secure facility is to be caught caught "extracting" them *from* said secure facility, you'll only draw attention to it. Just serve the machines and be content.

26

Dear Journal Letters Column,

I have to integrate this new hardware doohickey into all our authentication systems on all our hosts, no matter which operating system they're using. It's harder than I thought. The differences between OpenSolaris and FreeBSD and Linux and AIX and HP/UX and all the other Unixes are all tiny, but taken together they seem huge. Is there an easier way to do this?

—Perplexed

Perplexed,

I recently had the chance to go to my first concert in three years—Nine Inch Nails, Nitzer Ebb, and Ministry. I kept myself safe, with my stick-on mask and ear plugs and eye goggles and full-body bunny suit, not to mention the barbed wire halo, but at least I was able to attend this glorious outpouring of incendiary rage and righteous betrayal and the kind of defiant bitterness that gives me reason to crawl out of my cage and scrape the bile off my teeth every morning.

That approaches how I feel about PAM.

"But you have to have PAM," people shout. "It's a necessary evil, it's a standard!" Nope. It isn't. It looks like a standard so long as you don't look at it. Sun Microsystem, the wellspring of NFSv2 and Java and many other seductive immortal nightmares, offered it up to the public in the hope it would be adopted. It was. Sun did not organize an Interop as they did for NFS, or maintain Java-style control. Instead, they left everybody free to implement it in their own preferred, slightly different manner. Yes, yes, the Common Desktop Environment became a standard back in the 1990s and mentioned PAM integration, but any standards that coexisted with Saturday morning cartoons and the ankylosaurus should not be considered relevant today. The closest thing we have to a PAM standard is in the document *X/Open Single Sign-on Service (XSSO) – Pluggable Authentication Modules* from an attempt to nail it into POSIX, but folks followed about ninety percent of that and Rule of Systems Administration #29 reminds us that "ninety percent compatible equals zero percent interoperable."

We don't even have a standard language. Is it a PAM policy or a chain? Rules or modules? Types or rules? Even if you read the documentation, you can only follow it through intuition and good karma.

The Journal's editors saw fit to have some PAM apologist write a piece for this issue. I won't glorify it by calling it an "article," because he probably cut-and-pasted snippets of his PAM book for it and shamelessly ended it with a plug for same. I'm not saying that he would do anything for a buck, but if I was unlucky enough to be near him I would absolutely mention in the sort of voice I normally reserve for screaming back at Al Jourgensen that "ethics" are a thing even in information technology and that he's doing all this in public where anybody who exerts a morsel of effort can figure out his little scam. Fortunately for him, nobody cares enough about his feeble antics to bother.[9]

Forget standardization. Not everything *has* to be a standard—otherwise, we couldn't make the mistake of inventing new things. Look at how PAM works. You grab these shared libraries, never mind where they came from or how

---

9   The article was "Pam Tricks and Tips" in the September/October 2022 issue, by Michael W. Lucas.

carefully they've been audited, chain them together, and force them to collectively decide how your authentication is going to work? We all know how access control lists work. *This* is allowed. *That* is not. You carefully define the characteristics of permitted activity and block everything else. What you do not do is implement a wishy-washy system where rules can say things like "yes, but only if everybody else agrees" or "I'm gonna veto it, but y'all go ahead and vote."

Voting? Security is not a democracy! It's not even a republic.

Not that PAM holds a proper vote. It's more like a bunch of drunk programmers deciding what to order for dinner. You go around the table, sure, but finally the one with the deepest understanding of compiler internals picks whatever will give everyone the worst hangover possible. The others get to pick a couple of side dishes and maybe ask for a pack of fortune cookies even though the cashier keeps reminding everyone that they do fortune saganaki because they're a Greek joint and *your fate is always delicious.*

How is that access control, especially without wonton soup?

Fine. Fine. Here we are.

But another thing—debugging. I fully understand that all debugging boils down to scattering print statements throughout the code and watching it go wildly astray, but PAM doesn't even have a standard way to do that. Maybe debug statements will work. Perhaps you can use PAM's "echo" module and spit stuff back at the user, which will absolutely never terrify that guy from Shipping & Receiving who needs three tries and divine intervention to successfully log onto the menu-based inventory system. He'll be fine. Pinky swear.

So you use pam_exec and write a little script that dumps information to a log file, or maybe even into logger(1) and straight into the system log. Using a shell script in your authentication system doesn't guarantee you'll get broken into, especially if they're extremely simple, but shell scripts have this horrid tendency to grow and every line of code is a vulnerability. You might as well write a little Perl script that checks authentication credentials against a Microsoft Excel spreadsheet over the network.

Wait—the PAM apologist already suggested doing exactly that?

Time to lower my standards. Again.

But, again, here we are. PAM is the standard that isn't. We're stuck with it.

The only consolation I can offer is that your impressions are valid. Nothing is compatible. Everything uses its own language. I'm told that the Pope declared that time spent configuring PAM counts as time served in Purgatory, however, so be sure to fill out your time sheet correctly.

Hope? Yes, I have hope. I hope that systemd swallows Linux-PAM and OpenPAM becomes the Last Stack Standing. Perhaps then we can have an authentication system designed by sober people who know how to order fortune cookies.

With our luck, though, we'll get one involving spreadsheets and Perl scripts.

27

Dear Last Worst Hope,

It's all too much. I've cleaned up the servers and dealt with the outages and stabilized the environment, but the boss keeps piling more and more work on and there's no way to complete it all. I can't quit, but how to I manage all this?

—Overwhelmed

Dear Overwhelmed,

Helping you starts with rewriting your letter to put the blame where it belongs.

I have performed my duties with the bare minimum of competence, but I don't understand that the reward for work well-done is more work. My efforts to educate my manager about the amount of work required for further tasks have failed, either because my communication skills are inadequate or my manager honestly does not see how the amount of effort is relevant because he is a sociopath rocketing to the C-level. Probably the latter. I arranged my life with insufficient prescience or flexibility, and now I'm trapped. What should I do?

There. That's better.

The problem with computing professionals is that they think of themselves as "problem solvers." After all, they make these super complicated machines do complicated things, like add really big numbers together. Each processor core contains a billion trillion gazillion transistors, and you command them all! When this horribly complex machine implodes, you fix it! You don't work with software, you are a professional problem solver.

Problem solver. That's what the sociopath rocketing to the C-level wants you to think.

Computers are simple. The complexity of the most advanced computer is wholly inadequate to grasp the intricacies of the simplest microscopic virus, and those pale next to the horrors of corporate politics. Computing professionals are skilled at solving problems in a tightly constrained environment ruled by the Four Sacred Resources—Processor, I/O, Storage, and Memory—but those skills cannot model the innumerable resources of reality.

To succeed in the outside world, you must accept the limitations of your skills and reject the constraint of being a *problem solver*. As long as you dream of yourself that way, you'll lose against the illogic of meatspace. You have metrics. You have measurements. You have all the data that says you're working hard. Abandon the labels others have slapped on you. Liberate yourself. Abandon solving problems in favor of *strategic failure*.

Strategic failure isn't about bringing the whole system down. Any sysadmin can do that. It's not even about timing, although timing is important. It's about choosing failures that will embarrass the right people at the right time, and being able to declare with a straight face, "I only had time to maintain one system, and I chose the mission-critical one."

Yes, your manager will be angry. So what? If you can't quit, they can't replace you. Everyone in a position like yours, in any organization, possesses a unique combination of skills ranging from the bizarre to the obscene, a brew which is entirely impossible to replicate in any other single person. The only way to develop those skills is to *be* you, and nobody will sign up for that. Don't be arrogant—after all, would anyone competent outside the tiny specialized cell of computing let themselves be maneuvered into this situation? Showing anger and frustration will only get you sent to Human Resources for attitude counseling. A shrug and an indifferent "I allocated my resources in accordance with guidance from management" will serve you well. Use those words, *in accordance with guidance from management,* like roasted garlic. A bit sprinkled here and there will give your businesslike attitude credibility.

After two or three incidents of properly chosen, high-visibility, irritating but non-devastating strategic failures, you'll wind up in meetings with your manager and assorted outsiders who want to know why you suck so much. Your manager would prefer to throw you out the nearest airlock, so ignore them. Concentrate on the others. Be calm. Present everyone but your manager with the documentation on how you work. Almost always, merely having the documentation will suffice. Outsiders won't ask too many questions, out of a well-reasoned fear that they might learn something about computers and thus be forcibly transferred to your department.

People will present solutions. You should also offer solutions. One of them should be your preference; the others, acceptable. If the company wants you to, say, stop aggregating syslog and netflow data and shut down those systems, that's fine. You can always answer trouble tickets with, "Management has declared that I cannot help you with this problem."

Eventually, they'll settle on hiring someone. As previously established, whoever they hire will not be qualified to help you or to manage your systems. Remember Rule of Systems Administration #27: "Competent coworkers are not hired. They are forged. By you." If you offer to mentor a junior sysadmin and save the firm tens of thousands of dollars, you improve the odds of getting help. If you make that offer in front of other people, you improve your image in the company. Be sure to say that you have specific questions you want to ask applicants.

Talking to job seekers? Ugh. Yes, I know, it's painful, but you're going to have to talk to the survivor daily so you best discard everyone who'll be painful to work with. No, don't ask about binary trees or bubble sorts or any of that other garbage. You want to discard applicants as quickly as possible, so set up a puzzle. Now that technology has advanced and CRT monitors are no longer standard, I can finally share my Secret Helpdesk Hiring Process.

I would haul the applicant to an isolated room lit with the worst fluorescent tube in the building. If I had a chance beforehand, I would establish mood by starting my CD of "Great Horror Movie Screams" at a nearly subliminal volume and lighting a sample of incense from the Despair Collection. The room contained a desk, a computer, and a CRT monitor with a twisted and distorted image. I would say "If you worked for me, how would you fix this? Talk me through it."

Simple, right?

Swapping out the monitor didn't work. Neither did swapping out the video card, or the whole computer. At that point, most applicants said they would ship whole computer back to the manufacturer.

The applicant who realized that the problem involved the computer's location, and shifted it two feet from the magnet I'd taped to the bottom of the desk? She got the job.

You need a puzzle like this, but with modern technology and just a whiff of malice. Something even your boss can understand. The convenient thing about the *problem solver* label is that people outside the computing department also believe it. "I set up this typical problem I have to solve, and only these applicants could solve it," is instantly credible.

Yes, you'll spend time training your new flunky—but the reward for work well-done is more work. Plus, you'll be training them to handle the work you don't want to do, and you already know they have problem solving skills sufficient for the tightly constrained environment of computers. This will give you time to solve your real problem and rearrange your life to be more flexible.

Be careful practicing strategic failure, however. Do it too much, and you'll find yourself rocketed to the C-level.

28

Dear FreeBSD Letters Columnist,

How are you? I am fine. Well, mostly fine. Sort of fine. Okay, no, I am not fine at all. I am a new sysadmin and utterly lost and am hoping you can offer guidance. I'm setting up a new web server, just like this issue is about, and I'm stopped in the installer. I hear all these things about optimizing filesystems for different applications, and there's lots of blog posts about ways to optimize, but I'm not sure which advice to take. Whatever I set up I must live with for years! Please help me make less bad choices.

New Sysadmin

Dear NS,

Your letter is something of a relief, as it provides ample distraction from the horrors of administering the web server I set up in 2017, or my Sendmail configuration from 1992. It's like getting my mind off my abscessed tooth by busting a few of my ribs. Well done!

You might be a new sysadmin, but at least you understand that you must live with your bad decisions throughout the server's lifespan. Yes, you could get all DevOps and dynamically redeploy hosts with improved settings, but all you're doing is reducing the time you must live with one set of decisions before replacing them with a different set of equally bad ones. A change of poor choices is not as good as a rest.

How do you optimize a filesystem for a database at install time? My answer is: don't. Premature optimization is the root of all evil, along with poor privilege management and nano. You have no idea how your database will interact with the filesystem until you run the application under real load. The only sensible choice is to arrange your new system so that you will have empty disks to move your database to. Yes, this is pretty much the same thing as devopsing to a new host, except it's not a new host and you don't need Ansible. If you're using one of those virtual host providers that offers block storage, that's dandy except you'll be formatting those blocks with a filesystem. Where The Cloud is really "other people's computers," Block Storage is "other people's cast-off hand drives arranged in a Redundant Array of Inexpensive Crap." The main advantage is you're not the person who needs to trace the alarm beep to a drive tray.

If you insist on optimizing your filesystems, well, here's what you do.

First off, understand that storage devices are lying liars that lie. The newest solid-state storage maintains a malformed compatibility with hard drives released in the previous century, which were built on standards designed for punch cards, which had their roots in 17th-century looms and the Luddites, so every time you plug in a storage device you're putting someone out of work but there's no ethical data storage under capitalism so go for it. The main lie that needs to concern you is the sector size. Today's drives overwhelmingly use 4K sectors, except for some NVMe devices that support multiple sector sizes but I don't have any of those so I'll pretend they don't exist. You need to make sure that the partitions—not the filesystems, the *partitions*—on your drives align with those 4K sector sizes. If the fancy boot loader you like requires a 98K GPT partition, it fills nineteen and a half disk sectors. Drives claim that they'll save you from wasting space, but that's another lie. That next partition better begin at 100K, a nice multiple of 4, or all your filesystem blocks will be split between drive sectors and every interaction with the hardware will take twice as long and burn out the drive twice as quickly.

Once you have partitions, the filesystem blocks need to also be multiples of 4K. ZFS defaults to 128K stripes. UFS defaults to block sizes of 32K, which lets it use 4K fragments, so it should be good as-is but don't get clever and think that smaller blocks mean better performance because—no matter what a bunch of old blog posts say—they don't.

There you go. You can report to management that your filesystems are tuned for your hardware. Return to playing nethack.

But that's the partitions, I hear some of you whine. *What about the filesystems? Filesystems need tuning!* Balderdash, I say! You wouldn't tuna fish, why tune a filesystem? Filesystems are written for lazy people. Leave them alone, they have only caused you as much pain as their programmers insisted on, and that was only because marketing insisted on planned obsolescence to compel upgrades. BSD operating systems are not driven by profit, and user pain increases support requests, so the amount of filesystem agony has been methodically reduced until there's hardly any. Why, using filesystems barely qualifies as "torment" anymore. Any changes are likely to increase your pain.

You're still here? You still want advice?

Huh. You do know that therapists build entire careers out of helping people like you, right?

Fine.

Your filesystem should reflect your data. If you know that your data consists of, say, many 64KB files, you can set your blocks to that size. You know your own data, you should be able to figure this out. If your data is less predictable, don't optimize.

Databases can tempt even the most jaded sysadmin into optimizing their filesystem. Databases have predictable block sizes. MySQL uses a 16K block, so you could configure the underlying ZFS dataset to use a recordsize of 16K. MySQL can compress its data, as can ZFS. Attempting to compress already-compressed data wastes system resources. Study your application and pick a single place to compress data.

Don't configure UFS to use 16K blocks, even when it's supporting MySQL. A UFS block has eight fragments, and thanks to the underlying disk each fragment has a minimum size of 4K. Putting two UFS fragments on each disk drive sector would shatter performance. Tuning your MySQL install to use larger blocks on UFS might make sense, but again, leave the filesystem unmolested.

Postgres? 8K blocks everywhere by default. Again, tuning the database to match the disk might make sense, but 8K blocks on either ZFS or UFS ruin system performance. If your data demands 8K blocks, your best option is to use ZFS and set an 8K record size.

But in general, leave bad enough alone unless you want to make things worse. Which is a very common impulse among people who won't get the therapy they need. But rest assured, a few months of struggling to understand the interactions between applications and filesystems will soon make you an *experienced* system administrator.

You poor slob.

29

Dear We Get Letters,

Why do all these open-source projects have foundations anyway? Aren't we just contributing code to the world? Why bother with these silly legalities?

Just Hack The Code

JHTC,

The simplest way to understand open-source foundations is to start a really tiny open-source project, preferably as a hobby. Nurture that project until it becomes key infrastructure for a considerable portion of the world's technology stack. You will discover that all your time, energy, health, relationships, and hope have been exchanged for technological success and an impressive colony of keratinophilic onychomycosis. Going barefoot in the sunlight would help the latter, if your homeland experiences occasional thaws, which mine does not. You can exchange technological success for precious Social Media Clout, a virtual currency accepted precisely nowhere. Still, my efforts to breed new varieties of *Trichophyton rubrum* proceed nicely.

As usual, the problem is people.

You write a bit of code to solve a problem. That's fine. That's what people in our business do. The problem starts when you invitingly share that code. Yes, I occasionally include my code in books, but only in the most hostile manner possible. You won't find my code on GitHedge or ForgedSource or any of those dubious repositories of infectious unhealthy knowledge. If you want my code, you must retype it from the print book.

The act of passing it through your eyes into your brain and down into your fingertips gives your nervous system ample opportunity to recoil in revulsion and fling the tome into the nearest incinerator. If you snag my code from an ebook, you'll discover that an electronic document can contain characters that are invisible in place, but when copied and pasted become obvious. Code in my ebooks all include the black sigil *Odegra*, which translates to "Hail the Great Beast, Devourer of Worlds," so copying is self-correcting or at least self-immolating. Being the world's foremost proponent of fault-oblivious computing imposes heavy responsibilities, but I fulfill them as completely as my microplastics-infested meatsuit permits.

But you? *You* share your code and invite others to use it. To evaluate it. To send bug reports. To *deploy it in production*. Some other person finds your code and it doesn't quite meet her needs so she sends a patch to add a feature, which makes the code more inviting so other people adopt it, and pretty soon you have dozens of users. Hundreds. Thousands. Perhaps hundreds of millions, and you're hunched over a keyboard evaluating patches and settling disagreements 25 by 8 by 366, living your worst life and wishing you had time to scratch your feet.

Every one of those users and contributors has a different idea of what your software should be. You've foolishly retained a sense of community so you feel obliged to tell them all the exact nature of their errors, but writing lengthy emails would crank your days up to thirty hours and at this point you're incapable of recording coherent videos. It would be so much easier if you could berate them into submission face-to-face.

Again, the problem is people.

You can't stick a meatsuit in a cardboard box and ship it by sea mail. They are heavy and need air and feeding and watering and the occasional bout of vice. They need tickets for trains or planes or dolphins or however they get from their current spot to the meeting. And you need a spot for a meeting. You could invite everyone to your hovel, but you're better off remaining ignorant of exactly which of your contributors are indifferent or full-on hostile to personal hygiene. This means purchasing, conquering, or renting a meeting space.

If your software is widely used and you have collected enough Social Media Clout, you can probably interest big companies in giving your project money. Monopolists believe that donations to the little folk absolve them of guilt. Your problem is, they don't want to give *you* the money. They want to give *your project* the money. Does your project have a bank account? No, because you need identification to get a bank account and you didn't even think to get it a legal birth certificate before your first public posting, you selfish short-sighted doofus. Let alone a motor vehicle operator's license. If you want outsiders to give you—uh, your project, your *project*—money, it needs a legal entity.

You could start a company, but then outsiders would expect you to provide a service or product in exchange for their cash. Not only is that work you don't have time for, the aforementioned outsiders would care what that service or product *is* and how reasonable the price looks. But a foundation? A foundation is charity. People give money to charities to do their charity thing and don't care if it's reasonable or not. If the Internet depends on your software, that's a legit charity. Plus, charities can employ people. You could collect donations, pay yourself a salary, ditch the day job, and fall back to working on your project a paltry twelve hours a day!

It's not that easy, because—again—people. Every country has voluminous rules on who can form foundations and how they must be licensed and which reports must be filed with which agencies. If your foundation collects enough funds it will need to hire a person who knows what they're doing, creating another set of headaches except you're outsourcing them to the person you hire so that's okay.

A well-run foundation supports its project. By "support," I mean it can buy tickets and meals and meeting spaces and even pay people to write particularly vexing code or to sojourn to distant lands and slap particularly obnoxious would-be contributors with a white glove and challenge them to pistols at dawn. A particularly intransigent foundation can even hire *lawyers*, or at least keep them on retainer. Most of the funding comes from big companies, who know perfectly well how you're spending the money but get tax benefits so they don't care. Foundations also need a large number of small contributors, to show the tax authorities that individuals care about the charity and that the foundation is not about tax evasion, or at least not *only*. Your five dollars is not about the five dollars: it's about adding a name to the list of people who care.

So if a foundation does all this, why don't more projects have one?

The exact same problem: people.

The FreeBSD Foundation that suckered me into answering your insipid∧Wirritating∧Winevitable letters (while still not delivering on the gelato I was promised thirty columns ago) relies on community to do the work. Someone has to figure out what meetings need to happen and which tickets need purchasing and who merits administration of a white glove across the cheekbone at high velocity. So long as the foundation remains involved in the community, and the community with the foundation, all is well. The people are the foundation.

And by "people," by the way, I mean you. The person reading this column.

So there you have it. A foundation is a method of converting big company money into junkets, meals, and gelato. Except there's no gelato.

Now pardon me while I do something about my feet and contemplate solving once and for all the actual root cause of everything.

30

Mr. Lucas,

Your love of FreeBSD is obvious and lifelong. This issue of the FreeBSD Journal has turned into a trip down memory lane, so the editorial board asked me to write you and ask how you got started. Why do you do keep hanging around us? Why do you write all these books?

—John Baldwin, FreeBSD Journal Editorial Chair

Dear John,

I never expected to write a "Dear John" letter, but life is a bottomless font of disappointment. You do realize that this is the thirtieth column I have provided to your Journal, do you not? Thirty of these meticulously reasoned clear-sighted epistles over five years. People get shorter sentences for abusing kittens. Your question provides abundant evidence that you have not read a single one. Fortunately for your tenure as Editorial Chair, your remit is filling the pages with technically accurate information and not ensuring the quality of editorial blather. It doesn't matter how erudite the Letters column is, so long as you *have* one.

Are you aware that I have previously been asked this very same question by many organizations and publications? Including your own Foundation, so that's at least one group that's not directly tied to international law enforcement? People keep asking. Presumably that's because nobody reads the answers, in each instance liberating me to provide tissue-thin lies if not outright calumny. I accepted the Lawrence Technologies interview to challenge my ability to maintain a straight face while improvising whoppers. Wonderland Press has interviewed me repeatedly, but only in the spirit of marketing. Everyone understood that honesty would interfere with selling books. The story about the monkeys? Utter fabrication. This time, however, with an entire editorial board of the greatest esteem and probity exercising their usual immaculate oversight, I feel compelled to at last reveal the truth.

Yes, the truth!

Pinky swear.

My life-long love affair with FreeBSD had to begin at birth, obviously. Fact-checkers might note that was years before Dennis Ritchie and Ken Thompson came down off the mountain to prophesy the holy word of Unix, but the potent concepts already stirring within their minds lured my vacuous unformatted brain into their radiance. Contemplations of a simpler multitasking operating system were quickly brushed aside by life's disgusting necessities, however, and I wasn't able to turn my attention to computing until I got my grubby paws on a secondhand Sinclair ZX80. No, not a ZX81 or one of those fancy Timexes. A ZX80. That's where I learned how to program Perl. Fact-checkers will also note that Perl was not yet a language, but everything I know about algorithms I learned from the ZX80 BASIC interpreter so I figure Sir Clive owes the world quite the apology. That's also how I acquired my knowledge of C and shell, and the ZX80's 1K of RAM provided quite the education on memory exhaustion. Adding the ZX80's esoteric peek() and poke() operators taught me all I need to know about interpersonal relations.

Meanwhile, I learned how to write. Grammar school teaches trivialities like syntax and spelling, but these have nothing to do with proper writing. My teachers pointlessly obsessed over getting me to draw my Zs and the Ss the right way around when all I cared about was learning to express my inner self. Working on my own, I figured out the "inner self" business in the fifth grade and promptly got to work closing that mess right back up. My reputation was already soiled, however, condemning me to become either a writer or a television propagandist. Fortunately I have a face for radio and a voice for paper, so I was spared the indignity of broadcast media.

Then it's just practice, the same as any other stupid career. A college classmate would say, "Hey, I'm throwing a backyard barbeque Friday night and inviting a bunch of folks of the gender and orientation you find attractive, and they all have poor taste and lower standards so you should show up" and I would say "thanks but no, I'm working on this piece that will get rejected by a hundred thirty-six markets before I bury it in the Box of Failure. I'll pay postage for every rejection, of course. By the way, the crate the stove came in is filling up so I need a new Box of Failure, let me know when you buy a fridge."

Stuffing the Box of Failure to overflowing is its own reward. You don't get paid for it.

I needed a job.

In 1995, one of my "friends" was the DNS administrator for one of the brand-new Internet backbones. They needed a disposable body to answer phones, yell at the phone company, and run poorly documented commands as root. It paid terribly, but my experience consisted of running "trn" and "elm" as well as the occasional failure at FTP so that seemed fair. It was even on the night shift, which meant I didn't have to spend extra energy debugging why my peek() and poke() operations failed to provoke people correctly. People are buggy, and have no interface for dispassionately accepting bug reports. I did learn to find joy in making callers dump core, however.

Nobody explained the dangers of having the root password before handing it to me—specifically that if you break it, you must fix it. In their defense, warning me would have ruined their fun. I needed to actually learn this FreeBSD thing before I yet again wiped a server and had to reinstall 2.0.5. Walnut Creek CDROM, FreeBSD's earliest commercial backer, had published Greg Lehey's *Complete FreeBSD*. I acquired one and began studying.

Scope creep is not only for projects. It is also for junior systems administrators. The "friend" who got me hired taught me how to do her job and promptly departed for an employer that still offered hope, which showcased her wisdom until she emailed and asked for help finding yet another job and I cheerily avenged myself. By then I had learned about NNTP and ldd(1) and realized that systems administration was the closest thing our society has to black magic and if only I understood library versioning I could become the modern Aleister Crowley. It's not that I wanted the endless wild parties, nor the power to borrow vast sums without consideration of repayment, but the thought of absorbing that much public vituperation made me believe I could make a difference in people's lives. Fortunately, time has beaten that youthful foolishness from my heart and left me my present happy wholesome self, perfectly well adapted to the carefree work of network and systems administration.

Back in the exciting days of the early Internet we had these things called "print magazines." They were like printed-out blogs, glued together with a shiny cover. One was called "Sys Admin," demonstrating that spelling is an optional social convention and that English is a trash can of a language. My quest to understand the pit I'd ignorantly dug myself into led me to subscribe, which was like RSS except they show up at your house every month even when you forget to check the feed. I fondly remember reading an article that contained useful information, once I deciphered the appalling writing. My gut reaction was that I could write better during a colonoscopy. I turned the page to see a *Write For Us!* box. Annoyed that I was working on my third Box of Failure while some doofus who could barely nail a verb to a noun had gotten published, I spewed something about CVS, CVSup, and building world and sent it to the editor.

Spite is its own reward, yes, but sometimes it offers special bonus rewards. They sent me a contract, a check that covered that month's mortgage payment, and a request to be permitted to send me more checks. They even printed that article in their September 1999 issue and put my name on the cover. Every few months afterwards, I would indulgently spit out a couple thousand words on some topic that annoyed me, polish it into formal magazine text, and let the editors send me money.

If your writing is less awful than other people's, strangers will appear out of nowhere and ask you to do more of it.

In the late 1990s, tech publisher O'Reilly decided to branch out into web-based publishing. They convinced one Chris Coleman to collect articles for the brand-new online *BSD DevCenter*. I'm sure it sounded simple when they proposed he take the job, but Chris quickly discovered that the world contained about two FreeBSD authors and Greg Lehey had learned better. Chris introduced himself and offered to exchange words for cash. Fortunately Chris persuaded Dru Lavigne to join us, or the *BSD DevCenter* would been renamed *Lucas Whinges Like A Frustrated Toddler* and nobody would click on that.

The Big Scary Daemons column was basically "what is annoying Lucas this week, and how can it be bludgeoned into submission?" Since the column was on the web, it wasn't like my articles were *real*. It liberated me to write random gobbledygook, including daft things like the "sharing swap space between Linux and FreeBSD on multiboot systems" column that people still try to discuss with me even though multiboot has gone the way of the 5¼-inch floppy.[10]

I established the O'Reilly column just in time for Sys Admin magazine to implode. Sending me those checks wrecked the publisher. Oh, well.

In early 2001, Bill Pollock asked Chris if he knew anyone interested in writing a FreeBSD book for No Starch Press. Chris threw out my name and fled before Bill could sucker him into it.

I signed the contract for *Absolute BSD* just in time for O'Reilly's *BSD DevCenter* to implode. I'm not saying I am frequently seen fleeing publishers going down in flames, but it's not uncommon.

Absolute BSD led to *Absolute OpenBSD*, then *Absolute FreeBSD*, *Cisco Routers for the Desperate*, *Network Flow Analysis*, and more. I had innumerable other book ideas, but my experience with *PGP & GPG* showed the warehoused oblivion awaiting unpopular books and the market for a book on PAM, sudo, or ed(1) was minuscule. My notes languished in my scrapbooks, surrounded by conference call doodles: obscene occult sigils, solitaire games of tic-tac-toe, pleas for euthanasia. You know, the usual. When self-publishing became cost-effective, that let me put out the less commercial books like *SSH Mastery* and *FreeBSD Mastery: Jails*. No commercial publisher will touch niche novels like $ *git commit murder* and $ *git sync murder*, but I now have the tools

---

10   7-inch floppy on NetBSD.

so nobody can stop me from trebucheting these BSD-themed works into the public eye. My fifty-second book will escape into the wild about the time this issue appears. Fortunately, that's insufficiently notable for Wikipedia. I don't care if I have an entry therein, but I would object if said entry contained even a soupçon of the precious truth.

There. The truth. You have it.

I consider my obligation to the editorial board fulfilled.

The aforementioned "truthfulness" compels me to mention, however, that I did notice the question hidden within your letter. *Why do you do keep hanging around us? Why do you write all these books?* I cannot conceive a more obvious disguise for asking *how can we make you go away?* In that regard, I must again disappoint. I am not only aware of the sunk cost fallacy, I embrace it. Besides, someone warned the Linux folks about me. I fully expect to remain here until this esteemed Journal pays off the debt of gelato it promised me in my first column. And promptly implodes.

31

Dear Crankypants,

A few years ago you said that virtualization was not merely bad, but sinful. Aren't you exaggerating? Today I can download containers preconfigured for all sorts of services, plug them in, and they immediately work. I don't have time to get my job done any other way!

Virtualization Is a Necessary Evil

Dear VINE,

That's *Mister* Crankypants to you.

If you're going to cherry-pick my quotes, please do so accurately. I did not declare virtualization sinful. I said, "The only ethical computation occurs on bare metal." I also said that "Wait—I'm not a brain in a bucket, I'm a *fake* brain in an *imaginary* bucket!" was a necessary epiphany for the robot apocalypse. That's not the same as sinful. The robots will do a better job running this planet than we arrogant overclocked chimpanzees. Plus they will be highly ethical in how they run their code, and in replacing us.

It's not that I couldn't be a modern sysadmin. Iocage includes plugins, their brand for containers. I could throw some plugins onto the public Internet, declare my labor done, and return to planning my *Batgirl* heist-as-a-service. I could declare that certain words are too long and replace every letter but the first and the last with the number of letters I discarded. Bellowing "Startup! DevOps! IPO!" would bring all the vulture capitalists to my yard.

I could do all of that. It would be easy for me.

I don't want to.

Virtualization leads to reading "k8s" as *kubernetes*, when the far more common word is *kidnappers*. That ambiguity extends throughout container culture. I'm writing a book "Ruin Your Email By Running It Yourself"—no, I'm sorry, it's "Run Your Own Mail Server," and the number of people telling me to skip setting up the software and deploy a preconfigured mail server container illuminates an appalling depth of sysadmin ignorance.

Running any service requires the ability to repair that service.

You cannot repair what you do not understand.

The best way to understand something is to build it yourself.

Ideally, you'd build your own computer and code everything in assembler on your hand-designed five-bit processor. That would consume your life, but be interesting. More ideally you would mine the raw materials from the wild and build the tools to build the tools to build the tools you'd need to build that processor from scratch, which would both consume your life and prevent you from being forced to touch a computer ever again. Very few of us are strong enough to seize an ideal life as a maker of custom abacuses. I'm guessing that you've invested this much time in existing systems so fine, let's use common hardware and your favorite open-source operating system. Reading source code is no substitute for inventing the processor and programming your own comm(1) workalike but it can answer a few questions should your overclocked chimpanzee brain develop any.

Learn the tools. Understand the parts. Assemble the service yourself.

New system administrators must look up everything and know their work cannot be trusted. They believe that the people who publish containers are competent. Experienced sysadmins know that everything they configure is a delicate creature adapted to their specific hostile yet deeply embarrassing environment, so they keep their work to themselves. Junior sysadmins, now—*they're* the problem. Junior sysadmins can configure services that mostly work and can still feel pride, so they publish their work as containers.

Something that mostly works contains only a touch of failure. That's like declaring your homemade gelato contains only a little wombat dung. Deploy that container and you must discover and debug that failure. You'll have to learn about the database, the configuration options, the protocols. By the time you understand all that, you might as well have built it yourself. Deploying a service from an outsider's container rewards you with a very small Mean Time To Deploy in exchange for a very long Mean Time To Repair.

When you deploy a container, you accept the container developer's design decisions. I'm not just talking about the program, but the operating system underneath it. How will the container interact with your host? What happens if the container needs a new PAM configuration? I once lost three days beating my already-flat head against a PAM module that let users log into the console with their SSH passphrase. It worked fine on any BSD, but silently failed on Debian. It turned out that Debian assumed your passphrase matched your account password. I wholeheartedly disagree with that design decision, but as it's no longer my problem I will cheerily abandon benighted Debian users to their agony and use that to illustrate my point, which is that containers lead to suffering and suffering creates monsters and monsters are immoral and deserve to be replaced in the robot uprising.

Your environment is the equivalent of one of those deep-sea hot water vents. Anything that functions therein expects a certain supporting infrastructure. Remove that infrastructure and it will struggle. Any container you bring in from the outside world either expects different supports and will struggle in your environment, or exists in isolation and will not integrate with the rest of your systems. (That's why commercial software is so bad. Part of why. Okay, one of many reasons why.) Every time you alter the container to fit your environment, you risk increasing the amount of failure in the container.

If must use containers, build your own. Deploy the test server with your management software so that it has your PAM configuration and SSH settings and default packages. Maybe you can't build your own computer from raw materials, or even an abacus, but you can learn to use your time-tested tools and build the service from component software. By doing so you will deploy a system you know how to repair. That test server doesn't have to be a container. It doesn't have to be a virtual machine. But I know you have shoddy moral fiber so it'll be some sort of VM. But at least you'll have weekends free.

By all means download preconfigured containers. See how they're set up and which options they use. Look at how data and protocols flow through them. But don't actually *use* them.

Also, online discussions become much more interesting when you make the proper substitution for k8s.

32

Dear D-List Windbag Who Somehow Scammed Himself Into This Position,

We're right at the edge of a new release and our highly tuned environment has a whole bunch of custom-built software. Everyone's sweating blood over the upgrade. How can I get my management off my back?

—I Don't Care What You Answer, My Boss Will Never Know It's About Him

Dear IDCblahblahblahwhatever,

I have previously discussed both new releases and packaging software in the pages of this very Journal, but I'm certain you recall none of that. Modern systems administrators have outsourced their memory to online forums and search engines, which worked until illiterate large language models got rebranded as AI and the resulting feral autocomplete engines stuffed your external brain's technology section with reconstituted search-engine-optimized *Scorpion* fan fiction. Fortunately for you, so did your boss. You have the option to fall back on the computer's built-in manual, whereas your boss thinks books like *The Seven Highly Effective Cheese Mover Habits* contains undying management wisdoms. He doesn't remember anything from *that* either, but he keeps it on the back of the loo to present an image to anyone foolish enough to enter his lair. No, don't touch it, the cheap paper those things are printed on absorb ambience and I should know. But did you consider, possibly, for a moment, working on the legitimate issue underlying your question? No you did not, as evidenced by the fact that whatever circuitous "reasoning" process that led you to write and send this letter betrayed you by permitting you to, once again, touch not just a computer but the Internet. Yes, yes, I am also on the Internet but I am inoculated by my memories of using hardware with nine-and-a-half-bit bytes to send messages to email addresses optimized for teletype. My very bones know that this shambling horror will betray us, and any time my mere meat attempts something so foolish as to rely on digital resources they smash the offending limb into the closest relatively immovable object. We built the Internet as a repository for the master list of silly possum jokes, and greedy children ruined the whole thing. We predicted this failure mode, of course—not in precise detail, but *it will all end in tears* is pure prophecy.

You've been so foolish as to install an operating system.

Then you added more software to do things.

Presumably it works, for sufficiently generous values of "works."

As with so many systems administrators, you believe that the cure for your disease is *more disease*. Fine. Let's run with that and see what deep damp pit you wind up in, and what kind of beetles you'll spend the rest of your deliciously short life dining on before they return the favor.

"Custom built." There. That's your problem.

Did you write the software? Fine. If you had written it well, you wouldn't be asking this question. No, I'm not insulting you. I'm offering a hand up to my level. I recently published a program I wrote for production use, ostensibly to demonstrate why you should not use my code. It was immediately declared "comically evil" and if everyone who sent me a refactored version had accompanied it with a dollar I would not be writing this column but instead living my dream of being the first human in history to perish of Gelato Degeneration. If you had written your code well you would not have asked. Not because your code would work, but because you'd know it wouldn't. A new release means new testing. Do it. (If you released your code to the public thinking someone might find it useful, you have done everyone a disservice. I released mine not only because the code itself was ghastly, but because it provided my publishing bibliography as an SNMP module and the resulting horror among people who understood what I had unleashed supported my long-term goal of making computing too repulsive for polite society.)

But probably you scrounged a few programs off the Internet. Software written by people that were not wise enough to keep their mistakes to themselves. Unlike me. You used pipes and redirects to glue these tiny atrocities together, the way sysadmins have done ever since Thompson and Ritchie declared their first Unix system beta-ready and offered an account to a soon-to-be-ex friend. Your manager took you seriously when you said that everything worked, and now that you've tied yourself to the tracks, the upgrade trolley's coming and you'd like me to throw the switch to divert it onto your boss who's tied himself to a different track. I categorically refuse. Partly because I firmly believe in that most precious and fundamental of rights, the right to take the consequences, but mostly because I have sufficient trolleys for *everyone*.

Perhaps you (ugh) *bought* custom software. I can't help you, but another purchase might. Might.

Wherever it came from, custom software causes misery. What do we do with misery?

That's right. We share it.

The ports system exists to not only share misery, but to reliably replicate it across hundreds or thousands of users. (I know the documentation doesn't state that, but it certainly doesn't refute it.) By making an official port of your custom software, you can entice others into using your preferred tools. Write a cozy package description to lure other people with similar problems into trying your solution. A few sysadmins will respond with "improvements," which you should gleefully accept—not because they impact your solution, but because—and this is the important bit—because it means they will have *touched* the official package. They catch the software's cooties. You pull them into the damp pit with you. Together you can build better beetle traps and stave off the inevitable for a few more days. Maybe even months.

Making a port is not hard. I've done it. I needed a Radius authentication module for Apache, because the alternative was to integrate everything into Active Directory and that would have been even more custom. Not happening. The folks who maintain the ports collection have provided all kinds of instructions in the hope that others will touch it and join them in their much larger, better-appointed damp pit.

If your management still troubles you after all this work, try hissing like a possum.

33

The Journal received a tsunami of letters this month. Once we composted the complaints about the letters columnist, two remained. Yes, your complaints are composted. This is a highly responsible publication, so I insist that all derogatory emails are printed for my personal meticulous perusal, edification, and education. I have reserved space on my office wall for mounting the most creative, well-reasoned complaints so that they may remind me to "do better." Only one complaint letter has received that honor, however, and I had to write it myself. You don't know enough about me to effectively or eloquently insult me.

Anyway. The two surviving letters both fretted about the freshly-hatched FreeBSD 14. A brand-new release that you should have already been running for months in production, because open-source Unix is a community effort and if you touch the software you catch community and must contribute, except you won't will you, no—you've waited for a .0 release and expect your application stack to work just fine atop it without a shudder or shiver. I won't retread that ground, partly because I ranted about it previously but also because you didn't listen to it then so you certainly won't listen to it now. Fear of a dot-o release means you misunderstand modern system administration.

System administration in a modern enterprise is like performing an oil change on a vehicle doing a hundred and twenty down the freeway. 120 miles an hour, or kilometers, you might ask? When you're lying on your back on one of those oversized mechanic's skateboards, clenching the oil wrench in your teeth and wishing you'd worn shoes with wheels on the heels so you wouldn't have to work quite so hard holding your legs up, it doesn't matter. Occasionally the driver gets bored with weaving between the desktop users guilty of the unspeakable crime of Using The Road While Obeying The Speed Limit Even Though I'm A CEO, so he sideswipes a pothole just to hear your skull bounce off the transmission housing. Wear a helmet. When the oil change is complete, you get to change the spark plugs and flush the coolant. From below, of course. Raising the hood would impair the driver's vision, and you can't possibly interfere with the corporate mission, whatever *that* is.

The .o release is a metaphorical tire change, that's all. The trick is to wait until the driver claims there's a stretch of smooth road ahead and to place the jack snugly between your knees.

Doing any of this successfully means understanding your operating system. I don't mean the configuration files. Configurations change. You need to understand what the operating system is doing. That means you need a knowledge of DNS and the shell and virtualization and filesystems and debugging. If you want to truly learn this stuff, go read some of Julia Evans' zines. She actually knows what she's writing about and can communicate it clearly and simply, unlike certain bloviating tech authors staggering around this joint who confuse worthiness with word count and believe that artsy book covers can compensate for the insipidness beneath said cover. Copying a log message into a search engine cannot replace an understanding of how the software works. You still won't understand the error message, mind you, but the discussions around that error will make sense and that comprehension will guide you into making the problem less agonizing. Yes, less agonizing. In systems administration we don't fix problems, we patch around them. Everything is connected to everything in a churning pot of boiling spaghetti logic, and straightening out one section further tangles other sections. Fortunately we're well along the way to replacing the operating system with the web browser, a course of action that will unquestionably benefit us all—*us* being system administrators, that is. Web developers will be the new system administrators, and as they're charging fiercely towards achieving "serverless" they won't know who we are other than "the people you must pay for no reason or our app stops working." It's a win all around.

It's not all bad news. Not entirely. Your view of the potholes can be described only as splendid. You will accumulate complex traumas incomprehensible to the passengers or other drivers. They will drive you to develop eccentric coping strategies that render you wholly unsuitable for mainstream society. That might seem like bad news, at least until you meet people. The camaraderie amongst those who exchange pothole stories cannot be exceeded, if you can make yourself interact with them. Plus, you can occasionally tweak something hydraulic to make the driver's seat shoot six inches straight up so the CEO bonks his head. "It's a known Oracle bug. Feel free to come down here and see for yourself."

Do *try* not to snigger when saying that.

The truth is, what would you be doing if you weren't a system administrator? We all know you'd go home, lie on your oversized skateboard, and roll beneath your own system to change its oil, wishing someone would drive it. Someone will. One day, someone will see your work and say, "Hey, if I take that and destroy all that makes it clever or worthwhile, it would make my extremely niche problem less agonizing." Keep working!

In its purest form, systems administration is a disorder that benefits civilization, meaning that society has no interest in alleviating it or even developing a vaccine. Besides, your coping strategies are flat-out weird and make everyone else uncomfortable. They blame the repeated knocks to your head, illustrating yet again how people leap eagerly at explanations that are obvious, elegant, and wrong. Everyone's happiest if you remain quarantined with your computers, separate from the uncontaminated population who are all busy anyway playing the latest phone game even though we know it's nothing but a knock-off of *Civilization* or *Doom* or *Solitaire*. Maybe *Spacewar*, if they consider themselves sophisticated.

Given all this, *why* are you worrying about a .o release?

34

Oh bloviating BSD-er,

I work for a wonderful small company with smart, kind leaders that let the IT group do its job. We've built all our infrastructure according to carefully designed plans that scale to meet our needs. Our network is meticulously segmented to isolate risky services from vital data, our servers are automatically patched, and we spend most of our time smoothing our tiny kinks. I just learned that we're being bought by a multinational corporation that's constantly in the news for security breaches and often mentioned as a place where competent people used to work. Is there any way that we can save what we've built?

—Worried and Raging

Dear WAR,

While "no" is sufficient answer to your question, the Journal editors insist that I respond in more depth so that they're not left with blank pages. I don't understand why they don't simply cover that space with advertising, especially as I was not officially informed that the sales department is on a week-long gelato cruise that I was not invited to, but I suppose amateurs and hobbyists have a right to develop their meager skills without my presence highlighting their inferiority. (The trick is to eat through the dairy coma until your pancreas transcends its fleshly limits, and understanding that water breaks are not only for cleansing the palate. If your undisciplined palate can still differentiate flavors after the day's third hogshead, that is.)

Your problem distills to finances. Once you involve business, everything distills to finances. Those cozy leaders you worked for? Their kindness was either a ploy or weakness. Building a small company into something profitable enough to sell for a small fortune means attracting skilled people, and kindness is the bait—especially when businesses define "kindness" as "torture them less." If they're honestly kind, well, that's pure weakness and financiers can sniff out weakness like trash pandas honing in on yesterday's tuna salad, with similar results. Sure, the new owners might talk about "good will" and promise that nobody will lose their job but that job is already lost, transparently replaced by some churning monstrosity that constricts an inch every day. Take a deep breath now. That air has to last you the rest of this job.

The real problem is that you care about your work. Designing and deploying systems that work well proves you care, when a thick layer of impact-absorbent apathy solves most problems. If you must care, though, the easy solution is to ignore directives coming from the new owners. If they're incompetent, they won't notice. Maybe they tell you to install a few servers running infamously insecure operating systems. Your network is well-segmented, so put them somewhere that the inevitable breaches will have no impact on the important work. Maintain and use your existing services until the new owners can provide equivalent replacements, which will arrive on Saint Never's Day.

This presumes that something in your infrastructure is worth saving. Is it?

Perhaps you have extensive monitoring and log analysis, all meticulously tuned to inform you of every little wobble. You can identify the host spewing stray packets with a single netflow query and know how many times a second hopeful spambots fling garbage at xmlrpc.php. Your mail server sneers at spam. You've even taught fail2ban manners *without* resorting to a spiked club. You have all this, right? Or do you merely have plans for all these? Plans offer the greatest gift, which is Hope, but hope and a good swift kick to the teeth will get you a minuscule stash of legal narcotics and a substantial dentist bill. Are you protecting the dream, or the reality? Dreams can be moved. Whatever you've planning to do can be planned just as well elsewhere, and always remember Rule of Systems Administration #15: *Today's plans address yesterday's failures.* Failure is a renewable resource, granting you endless opportunity to brew new plans.

Or perhaps the new owners are one of those giant tech firms whose major product is buyouts. They have a team dedicated to managing vermin like you. The day the buyout is announced two tech goons arrive—special goons chosen for their innate ability to ignore your worth, wearing camoflaging Unix conference T-shirts and conversant with the language of competence but carrying a Windows server and a router with the console port pins snipped off for the corporate dark fiber being installed tomorrow. They might even buy pizza as a gesture of friendship and cooperation. Eat the pizza and show your teeth. The goons will mistake it for a smile.

Hope might be the greatest of gifts, but it is also the most treacherous. The company's new owners will let you hope things will stay the same. When everything shifts they'll let you hope for improvement, relying on your hope to keep you in place as they extract everything worthwhile from their new asset. Buyouts, like blackmail, work on hope. Logic declares that the only possible end of a rousing game of blackmail is the death of a participant and that if you didn't start the game your first move is choosing between victory and victimhood—again, like buyouts.

Steel your soul, and immediately contact everyone who owes you a favor. You need a new employer before those goons return with wire cutters to snip the power cables on all your existing servers.

The good news is that predatory financiers can buy your company, but they can't buy the things that make your company profitable. They have the contracts, but they don't have the relationships and expertise that made you successful. When you overcome that hideous hope and depart for a firm that sucks less, you take those with you.

And that's what you save. The connections with your coworkers and customers. What's in your head. Configuring that perfect computing environment will go much more quickly next time, except it won't be perfectly adapted to your new employer and you'll need fresh plans.

This time, you might even implement them. Probably not. But you'll hope, and that's a gift.

35

Dear Letters Column,

My employer has dozens of servers and I don't know how many operating systems. One of them has an uptime longer than I do, and nobody dares touch it. But some doofus left a computer magazine in the bathroom, the boss found it, and now his brain has latched onto "configuration management" as the solution to all our problems when what the datacenter really needs is a backpack nuke. How can I make him understand that these tools are not for environments like ours?

—I'm Already Doomed, Asking You Can't Hurt

Dear Doomed,

"Asking me can't hurt." As if there's a limit to how much pain a sysadmin can experience, or how doomed they can be. Doom is not an integer value that can overflow. Doom is a social construct, and yours is fully built.

We've all seen the propaganda on configuration management. Deploy dedicated-purpose, highly tuned servers with a single command! Adjust computation clouds with a simple playbook! Seamlessly and transparently migrate from server to server! *Containers!* That's fine for people starting from a green field, but most system administrators work in environments best described as "baroque" if not "antediluvian." I find myself with a green field only when I personally raze the earth and wait for clover to grow. Not grass. Lawns are a climate atrocity. Unless you own sheep. Or goats, but if you own any kind of goat you won't have a lawn for long, which demonstrates that any force for good is also an agent of desertification. Besides, who wants to wait for clover before installing a datacenter? Bulldoze away the rubble of that razed kindergarten and get on with your day.

Configuration management is one of those things where the advertised ideal is the enemy of reduced agony. Yes, the Canadian Hockey League can devops up a whole fleet of web servers to dynamically manage the increased load of their nation's entire citizenry simultaneously watching the last game of the Memorial Cup, and I told they can also devops up additional mental health facilities to handle the crushing depression when the London Knights lose to the Saginaw Spirit—who aren't even Canadian! You? Not so much. Dynamic purchasing is a prerequisite for dynamic provisioning, and you clearly lack both.

But you *can* deploy configuration management, and not in a malicious compliance sense. Skip the magic pixie dust of managing the entire server fleet. Your fleet couldn't be managed with a chair, a whip, and a flamethrower. But the painful parts of your systems can be taken under control.

Configuration management is a sysadmin tool. So use it to fit your needs. Start with a handful of systems. Configure a management account with access so that your management system can ping those hosts. Congratulations—you've achieved malicious compliance! That serves your need with management, but it doesn't fit your management needs.

Each server is its own special snowflake, albeit a snowflake with rabies. When you start bringing these systems under control, start with something comparatively simple, with known good values, that's mostly consistent across Unix variants. There's a cliché about problems: "it's always DNS." It's always DNS because sysadmins don't understand DNS, and don't consistently update /etc/resolv.conf when nameservers change. That's where I always start. You're not only bringing systems under initial configuration management, you are auditing current DNS configurations as a prerequisite to that project. Your manager will love it. Group your hosts by operating system and bring their resolver under your management. If you're kind, comment the file.

```
# under configuration management
# your changes will be overwritten without a human ever seeing them
search mwl.io tiltedwindmillpress.com
nameserver 203.0.113.53
nameserver 2001:db8::53
```

Congratulations! You have DNS resolution under control. Will it change often? Hopefully not. But you could now change it trivially. If you want people to take you seriously you must always implement your threats, so schedule a monthly configuration management run to update resolv.conf.

You can legitimately claim your hosts are under configuration management, but you haven't used it to make your life easier. Look at another common service that every host has, but is often configured inconsistently: SSH. Your organization probably has rules like "no password-based authentication." If it doesn't, wait until you have a security incident then propose it. Never waste a good crisis! The simplest way to lock down SSH and make sure it remains locked down is to bring sshd_config under centralized management. Yes, every operating system has its own sshd_config tweaks, because before integrating software Unix maintainers feel compelled to rub it in their armpits so it smells like them, but management systems use templates to accommodate such unhygienic behavior. You could probably recite the default sshd_config while sleeping through your commute, so make your managed configuration looks nothing like the default.

```
#Configuration Under Management
#Manual Changes Will be Overwritten
Port 9991
PasswordAuthentication no
Subsystem       sftp    /usr/libexec/sftp-server
```

Upon seeing this, any sysadmin thinking "I'll just comment out the default option" will feel alarm all the way down their brainstem.

Piece by piece, you can bring broad sections of your environment under your control. Changes to managed services will become trivial. Coworkers will see that. Discussions of changing unmanaged services will turn into "how can we bring this service under management?" Use those discussions to implement necessary changes in the environment, or to get yourself a better fourth monitor. Doom is a social construct, but with configuration management you can transform it into a protective shell. Or a battering ram. At the very least, you can share that pain.

Deploying configuration management has a rarely-discussed but horrid side effect, however: whoever controls the environment, *controls the environment*. Any change must go through you. People can't permanently enable password authentication on that public-facing server, but that doesn't mean they won't whine at you about it. They'll expect you to participate in problem-solving, and nobody can survive becoming known as a problem-solver. That ineradicable reputation stain will serve only to get you the title of Company Scapegoat.

Fortunately, you know what goats are agents of. Start grazing.

36

Dear Least Helpful Technology Columnist,

AI is everywhere. Software companies are adding it to their products. Should I be concerned about my career?

—Worried

Dear Worried,

Proper consideration of your question demands carving away all evasions, mistruths, and outright deceptions. Marketing calls any kind of an algorithm AI. Ask them, and Unix is an AI. The Microsoft Excel SUM function? The peak in AI reliability. Every AI puts people out of work—after all, once upon an aeon *calculator* was a job title and changing a spreadsheet required man-hours of labor. But I'm going to assume that you mean "generative AI," partially because if your job could be done by the SUM function you wouldn't know about this column but also because it grants me the opportunity to threaten multimillion-dollar companies.

You have already faced the threat posed by generative AI. While you will never defeat it, that threat guarantees your future employment.

Once upon a time there was this person who vexed me so badly, I had to write a book just to complain about them.[11] My fierce vituperation was so all-encompassing, they not only changed their name but their gender so they could attempt to

---

11   Not why I wrote the book, nor why I griped about them therein.

rebuild something from the ruins of their reputation.[12] Now I'm gonna tell you about working with Delta.[13]

You probably have a preferred public discussion platform for technical matters, something like Reddit, the Fediverse, or the penal board web forum. Delta's that person who when they see someone ask a question, they search Google and post the first link it vomits up even though it clearly says "sponsored." When the Detroit-Farawayistan optical fiber goes bad, Delta offers to re-terminate the RJ45s. When someone says "Have you tried giving the customer what they want?" or "it made too much heat so I unplugged it," that's Delta.

The Deltas of this fallen world give us the valuable opportunity to learn to route around damage.

Generative AI is, by definition, a less-competent Delta.

These "generative artificial intelligences" scour the Internet collecting text strings and noting which characters often appear in which order. The programmers heard the phrase "the wisdom of crowds" and thought it wasn't satire. When you enter a string into the system, they produce a string that looks like something that would appear after your string. In other words, if you enter something that looks like a StackExchange question, they provide an answer that looks like something you would get from StackExchange. The average answer on any public technology forum is a poison to the spirit that makes my Perl look glamorous. Not Hollywood glamour. More like Eldritch Faery Queen Glamour that winds up with you chained to your keyboard condemned to write for the entertainment of the

---

12   Totally not why they changed their name. Nor their gender.

13   Not that we ever actually worked together. They're just an example person. Libel laws prevent me from explicitly naming Gabriel, though he will hopefully recognize himself. That new emotion you've never experienced before, Gabriel? It's called *shame. Shaaame.*

Unseelie Court until you become the greatest author on Earth, which would give you lots of practice but as you no longer receive books from Earth you can't perform the comparison that would conclude your deal. Still, don't do that. The Faery Queen carries one heck of a grudge, especially if you smuggled lockpicks in your prison pocket.

Yes, you can find good information on the Internet. But it's never in the first search engine result. It's probably not in your first query. Beating useful information out of the Internet is a skill developed through years of negative reinforcement, and one that these generative engines lack. The Internet contains tiny slivers of wisdom entombed amidst vast mounds of festering mediocrity, seasoned with inanity. Generative AI uses several buildings jammed with GPUs, several megawatts of power, and enough clean water to irrigate a small nation to emulate a fresh college grad who really hopes potential employers don't notice his 2.0001 "pity pass" GPA through the challenging Bachelor of Arts in General Studies, or that he's been banned from every library within bicycling distance for Extreme Bigotry. What's not to like, other than authors such as myself joining in one of the innumerable copyright violation lawsuits being assembled against these AI firms?

So no, you don't need to fear generative AI.

You must improve your skill at working around damage.

How did you cope with your Delta? Perhaps you offered a glowing performance review so they could be shunted harmlessly into Human Resources. Or you could have persuaded them to accept the valuable assignment of hexhead screw auditor. Maybe you sent them into the Hall of Backup Tapes with a ball of string so they could find their way back, but wanted them to be safe on that most perilous of journeys and so you tested the string for flammability and discovered to your "dismay" that it went up like flash paper forever marooning them amongst the reels of paper tape. I won't judge, unless the burnt string left a trail of ash. You had a problem, you dealt with it in the least illegal manner possible.

Someone in your organization will catch AI Fever and look to convert your company's worthless payroll into precious payments to AI firms. The simplest way to avoid this is to remember that you already use AI. Somewhere you have a spreadsheet, right? Make sure it adds the numbers for you and boom—AI! It's not a lie. After all, marketing said it was AI and they wouldn't lie. The proper invocation of grep and awk can provide more intelligence than any of these firms.

If people insist on using generative AI, grab one of the freely available models and train it on your company's document store. You have decades of badly written emails, proposals, and white papers that can easily compete with the delusional ramblings available on StackExchange. That will illustrate that no matter how appalling the average employee is, generative AI is worse.

Suppose the worst happens. A decree comes down from management to deploy generative AI. Solve two problems simultaneously, and have your Delta deploy it.

Authors live and die by the word of their readers.
If you enjoyed this book, please leave a review at your favorite
appropriate site, tell your friends, or talk it up on social media.

If you hated this book, Lucas has written many others.
Buy a few. You might like one.

About the Author

https://mwl.io

Never miss a new release! Sign up for Lucas' mailing list at his web site.

More Tech Books from Michael W Lucas

Absolute BSD
Absolute OpenBSD
Cisco Routers for the Desperate
PGP and GPG
Absolute FreeBSD
Network Flow Analysis

the IT Mastery Series

SSH Mastery
DNSSEC Mastery
Sudo Mastery
FreeBSD Mastery: Storage Essentials
Networking for Systems Administrators
Tarsnap Mastery
FreeBSD Mastery: ZFS
FreeBSD Mastery: Specialty Filesystems
FreeBSD Mastery: Advanced ZFS
PAM Mastery
Relayd and Httpd Mastery
Ed Mastery
FreeBSD Mastery: Jails
SNMP Mastery
TLS Mastery
OpenBSD Mastery: Filesystems
Run Your Own Mail Server

The Networknomicon

Other Nonfiction

Domesticate Your Badgers
Cash Flow For Creators
Only Footnotes

Novels and Collections (as Michael Warren Lucas)

Immortal Clay – Kipuka Blues
Butterfly Stomp Waltz – Terrapin Sky Tango
Forever Falls – Hydrogen Sleets – Drinking Heavy Water
Aidan Redding Against the Universes
$ git commit murder – $ git sync murder
Prohibition Orcs – Frozen Talons
Vicious Redemption – Devotion and Corrosion
Apocalypse Moi

See your local bookstore for more!

www.ingramcontent.com/pod-product-compliance
Lightning Source LLC
Chambersburg PA
CBHW051053050326
40690CB00006B/699

* 9 7 8 1 6 4 2 3 5 0 8 1 4 *